JUN 1 2 2

P9-DTA-610

"Few challenges of parenting are more daunting than dealing with an angry teen. Having experienced moments like the ones that Mitch Abblett describes here, I can relate to the periodic clouds of utter hopelessness, despair, and frustration that arise when our deep love and devotion to our children is challenged by their behavior and their emotions. This book not only provides a rational and scientifically grounded framework for understanding the often mystifying and bewildering expression of teen anger, but it pairs that understanding with the deep and timeless wisdom of mindfulness practice that can allow us to step outside the anger cloud and maintain some presence to reconnect with ourselves. By practicing mindfulness, we can reclaim our compassion, our inner wisdom, and the practical skills that Abblett teaches here."

—**Steven D. Hickman, PsyD**, executive director of the University of California, San Diego's Center for Mindfulness; executive director of the Center for Mindful Self-Compassion; clinical psychologist; and associate clinical professor at the UC San Diego School of Medicine

"This gem of wisdom from Mitch Abblett is about way more than teen anger. Mitch wisely recognizes that the openhearted quality of your own unconditionally loving presence is the greatest gift that you can offer your teen. By starting with cultivating your own embodied mindfulness, this book guides you toward the kind of authentic and transformative relationship with your teen that every parent aspires to."

—**Dzung X. Vo, MD**, pediatrician, adolescent medicine specialist, and author of *The Mindful Teen*

NAPA COUNTY LIBRARY
580 COOMBS STREET
NAPA, CA 94559

"A compassionate, easy-to-read book providing practical guidance while supporting parents who are almost certainly suffering along with their struggling teens."

—**Mark Bertin, MD**, developmental pediatrics; author of
Mindful Parenting for ADHD

"*Helping Your Angry Teen* offers clear, useful tools for parents, therapists, and other caregivers to help the angry teenagers in their lives. Adults new to mindfulness might find the tools developed by Mitch Ablett to help angry teens feel better will help them feel better, too."

—**Susan Kaiser Greenland**, author of *Mindful Games* and
The Mindful Child

Helping Your *Angry* Teen

How to Reduce Anger and
Build Connection Using Mindfulness
and Positive Psychology

MITCH R. ABBLETT, PhD

New Harbinger Publications, Inc.

Publisher's Note

This publication is designed to provide accurate and authoritative information in regard to the subject matter covered. It is sold with the understanding that the publisher is not engaged in rendering psychological, financial, legal, or other professional services. If expert assistance or counseling is needed, the services of a competent professional should be sought.

Distributed in Canada by Raincoast Books

Copyright © 2017 by Mitch R. Abblett
New Harbinger Publications, Inc.
5674 Shattuck Avenue
Oakland, CA 94609
www.newharbinger.com

Giving Effective Instructions Therapy Module adapted from *Modular Approach to Therapy for Children with Anxiety, Depression, Trauma, or Conduct Problems* by Bruce F. Chorpita and John R. Weisz, copyright © 2009 by PracticeWise, LLC. Used by permission.

Problem-Solving Therapy Module adapted from *Modular Approach to Therapy for Children with Anxiety, Depression, Trauma, or Conduct Problems* by Bruce F. Chorpita and John R. Weisz, copyright © 2009 by PracticeWise, LLC. Used by permission.

Cover design by Amy Shoup

Acquired by Jess O'Brien

Edited by Amy Johnson

All Rights Reserved

FSC
www.fsc.org
MIX
Paper from
responsible sources
FSC® C011935

Library of Congress Cataloging-in-Publication Data on file

19   18   17

10   9   8   7   6   5   4   3   2   1   First Printing

To my father, a patient worker of wood and an example of craftsmanship in parenting, an ability we need as we help our children toward their potential.

To my mother, a lover of dancing and a reminder of the grace required to weave love and compassion into the many moments of raising children.

Contents

Foreword

I live in Boston, a city with one of the highest densities of therapists in the country, and travel to conference after conference, meeting therapists of all stripes. Here's what I've found: there are very few really bad therapists, very few really good therapists, and many well-meaning but mediocre therapists. Not bad ones, mind you, and not dumb ones either—almost all have great ideas, passion, and solid credentials.

I've met family therapists who can talk a good game at a conference, who can throw around jargon about neuroses and complexes, but don't do much for you or your kid. I know therapists whom kids love to see but who struggle to make concrete recommendations to parents. And I know therapists who hand out sticker charts and reward systems that just end up in the family recycling bin. Then there are the therapists whom parents love but with whom kids sit in stonewalling silence for fifty minutes straight during one-on-one sessions. I've met plenty of prescribers with Ivy League diplomas who hide behind their prescription pads in the face of angry teenagers and hopeless families.

I've also read dozens of parenting books in my own quest to be a better therapist, meditator, writer, or parent, books that could have been boiled down to a few PowerPoint slides at best. To be honest, there are only a handful that I would recommend beyond their introductions—and I know hundreds of hopeless families hungry for help.

And then several years ago I met Mitch, read his first book, and heard him give a talk. We met up at a local lunch spot; we swapped stories about writing, teaching, therapy, and family. Five years later, Mitch is one of my best friends and a colleague and collaborator I respect above almost any other—especially when it comes to tough kids. Part of what makes Mitch special is that while he is smart (he does have the Ivy credentials) and has a toolbox of techniques, he doesn't turn away from the heat of family conflict. Rather, he marches in like a first responder, ready to face whatever comes his way. At the same time, he's a fully authentic human being who brings all of himself to both his own family and the families he works with. His warmth and charisma shine through even in his writing—no easy feat.

What you'll find in this book is Mitch at his best. Clear and compassionate, human and humorous, and most of all, eminently practical in his approach to dealing with angry teens. What Mitch offers are lessons in how you can be the best parent *you* can be for *your* teen, not the best parent according to someone else's five-step miracle recipe for a calm kid.

Little can feel more frightening than an out-of-control child raging at us. When anger burns over in adolescence, you may worry that your dreams for your teen will go up in flames too. What you'll get from this book is the wisdom and compassion to cool the flames of anger in your family, yourself, and your teen.

Mitch will challenge you—there will be work for you to undertake—but he will challenge you compassionately. And Mitch will never send you out there without first giving you what you need. The wilderness camp I attended as a young man (probably not unlike where some angry teens end up) had a saying: "There's no such thing as bad weather, just inadequate gear." Mitch will give you the gear you need to weather any storm with your angry adolescent.

In chapter 1, Mitch offers you the lay of the land, helping you to understand your teen, yourself, and your patterns as a family. In chapter 2, he gives you critical gear from mindfulness and positive psychology, and explains how to use it both on a regular basis and in emergencies. In chapter 3, Mitch offers you a map and explains how to chart your course forward while avoiding the dangers along the way. In chapter 4, Mitch hands you the reins and you learn the leadership skills you need to navigate your journey. Finally, in chapter 5, you and your family learn to empower each other, so that you can again enjoy the lifelong journey of growing together.

Happy reading! And more than that, may your family soon be happy again.

—Christopher Willard, PsyD
Cambridge, Massachusetts
author of *Mindfulness for Teen Anxiety*
and *Growing Up Mindful*

Introduction

When I buy a book—particularly one where I'm looking for help, support, or solutions—there are key questions I need answered right up front. I want answers to the "w" questions: Who is this book for? Why do I need this book? When will this book start to make a difference for me? I'm assuming the same applies to you.

Who: You're holding this book because you're an adult in a close relationship with an angry teen, and you want to end the unhealthy, upsetting patterns, the angry explosions, and the toxicity. Perhaps you're reading this to help a parent and child in your family or circle of friends. (For the sake of simplicity, I'll be writing as if all readers are parents. However, there's much here for family, friends, clergy, teachers, and clinicians as well.)

Regardless, you're invested in making the situation change. You're worried about the track events are currently on and the potential for complete, disastrous derailment.

Your teen does one or more of the following:

- Holes up in a personal space, emerging only for meals and money.

- Yells at the slightest comment you make, perceiving it as criticism.

- Has a history of aggressive or destructive behavior at home or elsewhere.

- Engages in high-risk behaviors, such as fighting, bullying, vandalism, or hanging out with the "wrong" crowd, and you don't seem to be able to have a single productive conversation about any of it.

- Has difficulty navigating a daily routine due to irritability and extreme moods, and every attempt by you to help is met by either shutting down or acting out.

- Engages in lying, acting out, and manipulative behaviors; this is eroding all trust and sanity in the household.

- Slings blame in your direction, often making no rational sense whatsoever.

If any of these apply, you're in the right place. If any of these apply, it's a sure bet there's a communication breakdown between you and your teen that's at least contributing—if not outright causing—much of the difficulty.

Where: Many of the parents I've worked with have tried it all—therapies with acronyms, cocktails of medication, token systems, time-outs, even hospitals and residential programs. They've traveled cross-town, if not cross-country, in search of solutions to help their angry, troubled teen.

This book is different than most of the others. This book doesn't ask you to go very far at all. Rather, this book asks you to go inside yourself and do some work there—and then use the results of that work in your communication with your teen. The where that's truly important isn't yet another therapist's or psychiatrist's office, and it isn't yet another outdoor challenge program (as helpful as these may be). Rather, it's where you and your teen already are.

My experience is that if you're willing to get fully *here* with your teen—to speak and act in the direction of where your teen really *is*—then things begin to improve.

When: It's a parent's lot in life to be preoccupied with the when of things when it comes to children. I'm sure you're thinking and feeling about how long things have been stuck for your teen and wondering when things will improve, or if they will at all. This book is based in mindfulness. So when will things start to shift? Let me put it simply and in just one word: *now*.

Why: It's not just that you want a bad pattern to end. You love your teen and want to truly *connect*. You want to form the authentic, loving relationship you anticipated on the day your child first entered your life. This book goes far beyond helping you manage tough behaviors and situations—problems—with your teen. This book delves deep into the heart of your relationship. It gives you the tools to bring back that connection—a connection all parents crave when they get past the pain and negative habits built up over time.

How to Put This Book to Work for Your Family

This book is organized in a clear, concise, and memorable structure to guide you and your teen out of the murkiest situations. The book is structured as five chapters. Chapter 1 provides an overview of anger in teens and introduces the PURE method of managing communication between parents and teens. The PURE method is a four-step sequence of mindful communication techniques. Chapters 2–5 are each dedicated to a single PURE step: mindful Presence, perspective and Understanding of behavior, Responsiveness to the situation at hand, and Empowerment of your teen and yourself. The PURE method guides parents to break toxic patterns of interaction with angry teens.

The PURE steps provide concrete, in-the-moment cueing about how to build effective, compassionate, direct, and authentic communication during tough moments at home. The PURE method, when practiced consistently over time, helps to "purify" parent–teen relationships that have increasingly become muddied by frustration and disconnection.

Beginning with a brief overview, each chapter explains, with anecdotes and examples, the PURE principle being highlighted. Each chapter guides you through the practice of specific mindfulness and positive psychology skills to use *online*—that is, during real-time challenging moments with your teen. In addition, each chapter provides *offline* suggestions to help you build perspective and a baseline mindful presence. These exercises, called Peaceful Parent Practices, help you develop an ongoing, deepening mindfulness and a compassion-focused daily practice. Common questions and sticking points are addressed in brief Ask Abblett segments dispersed throughout. Each chapter ends with a short to-do list.

In using this book, you have the opportunity to show your teen how you answer, "What is it we do in this family when things get hard and communication breaks down?"

Through your own example—through your willingness to practice the skills in this book—show your teen that what you do is you take care of yourselves and each other. This is one of the most powerful lessons possible you can teach your teen. Your teen is watching and will learn from your behavior regardless. What answer would you prefer your teen to see?

The strategies detailed in these chapters stand alone and can be used individually to produce benefits. However, at least for the first reading, I recommend that you progress through the chapters in sequence, as the skills you learn will build upon one another. It all begins with skills for establishing mindful presence—that is, your ability to be fully aware and non-reactive to your moment-to-moment experience as a parent. The PURE method for managing communication breakdowns with your teen works thanks to the presence you will maintain from the beginning to the end of tough interactions—that is, throughout steps one to four. Because of this, I recommend beginning with mindfulness and presence skills detailed in chapter 2. Have these well in hand before you move forward with the other chapters.

As you work through the chapters in sequence, I recommend that you continue to practice the skills you learned in preceding chapters. Appendix A, which is available for download at the website for this book (http://www.newharbinger.com/35760), offers specific recommendations for continuing to build these skills in a comprehensive way. Effective use of this book should feel like a rising wave of momentum. The goal is for the method to be portable and doable in a range of situations. By the time you reach the conclusion, you'll be ready to put it all together and use the entire PURE method in actual situations with your teen.

Finally, I recommend that you keep a journal of your efforts to improve your relationship with your teen. Writing things down will make your efforts more real and help you stay on track.

What Teens Want Most (But Won't Admit)

Before we get started building skills, it's important to consider not only the reasons *you* are working through this book, but also why *your teen* will be responsive to your efforts. We'll look later at some of the core whys behind your teen's problem behaviors, but before we do, let's pause to name the biggest one: it's all about *you.*

Among all the teens I've worked with over my years as a therapist, I've yet to work with any who were completely indifferent to their parents. No matter how much resentment and anger, how much disconnection and disdain a teen feels, a teen's strong emotions make it clear that parents still matter.

During my graduate school years, a supervisor once asked a group of us trainees what the opposite of love was.

"Hate," we said with confidence.

"No," the supervisor said. "It's indifference."

Teens often direct anger toward parents because parents figure large in their worlds. No matter how negative things may be, you are still attached to your teen. That connection is something to be built upon.

At times your teen's anger—and your own—will heat up. This book helps you build the skills to turn down the dial and keep interactions with your teen from reaching the boiling point.

1 Anger in Teens: The Problem and the Solution

So, you've considered all of the "w" questions of the introduction and are certain you're in the right place. Before we launch into the PURE method—its skills and strategies—you must first understand the nature of your teen's anger. Without the right conceptual hooks to hang your new skills on, your good intentions may simply fall by the wayside.

In this chapter you will:

- Develop your appreciation for the needs and possible mental health factors driving teen anger.

- Learn about the unintentional communication patterns between parents and kids that keep anger in the picture.

- Begin to engage in practices of mindfulness and positive psychology, and learn how these concepts are embedded in the PURE method.

The Ancient Context for Anger

Imagine trading in your living room, illuminated by the glow of its flat screen, for a fire-lit cave with a cold stone floor. You're a prehistoric human and a saber-toothed tiger is preying on your family. Without anger, what would you do? How would things turn out for you and your kin? What would happen to the human species?

For millennia anger has protected and sustained us against physical threats. Our brains evolved limbic, or emotional, processing structures to spark us to self-maintaining action—that is, to fight, flight, or freeze reactions. These have allowed us to survive dangers and persist through to the present day.

What if, as prehistoric humans, we sat cross-legged in a full-lotus position outside the mouths of our ancestral caves, meditating with eyes peacefully closed for hours on end? We might cultivate some presence, but that flame of awareness would soon be snuffed out. (Hungry tiger, anyone?). Without anger—without the fierce flailing of indignant energy to fight, to protect ourselves—in such a perilous world all that meditating would matter little.

While our capacity for anger is natural and necessary, it carries a price. Even though our modern world has largely traded curtly worded text messages for tigers, anger continues to ignite us to reactive action. Our brain's ancient architecture knows no difference. It thus shakes us with the same urgency. Yes, anger is natural. However, just because something is natural doesn't mean it's ideal. The modern mind needs mindfulness as a corrective antidote to what eons of evolutionary changes have trapped within our skulls.

Few contexts bring out the prehistoric urges in us like parenting. A few years ago, one winter morning before preschool, my daughter was not having the idea of wearing a coat.

"Celia, please put on your coat." I was running late—for a session in which I'd be preaching mindful parenting of all things.

"No," she barked. "I'm not wearing it!"

Cue the caveman within. Running late... My agenda... She's being ridiculous... Doing this yet again, on purpose... The thought parade trampled all semblance of presence from my brain.

"Put on your coat, Daddy's going to be late."

"No!" she screamed, flopping on the kitchen floor. The shoes I'd barely managed to jam on her feet flew across the room. "No coat!"

Remember, I teach mindfulness. I emphasize its importance to every trainee, workshop participant, and parent I work with. And that morning, I grabbed up Celia's coat, bent down close to her in the kitchen, and snarled, "Put on your fucking coat!"

She froze and allowed me to press the coat around her.

We were both quiet on the way to school. Usually Celia is a chatterbox, but that day, strapped into her car seat, she sat in atypical silence. A tsunami of shame crashed down on me. I, a mindfulness loudmouth, had let my anger f-bomb on my own daughter.

From the quiet of the backseat, Celia broke the silence: "But, Daddy?"

"Yes, Celia."

"Daddy, I don't want to wear my fucking coat." Her voice was as sweet as my guilt was sour.

I share this less-than-glowing testament to my own parenting because the evolutionary, brain-based reactive surge of anger appears to be universal. Anger is never going to leave you completely, nor will it ever fully leave your teen. However, anger need not be the toxic theme of your teen's life, nor of your relationship. There is a path for provoking change in your teen's brain. This book guides your journey along that path. Your journey starts with understanding the causal factors of your teen's angry struggle.

Where There's Smoke: What Sparks Teen Anger

Teens send parents messages through their behavior, especially their most off-putting, anger-laden actions. I organize these messages under the acronym RSVP—I'll explain what the letters stand for in a minute—because for parents, the key is to respond (or RSVP) to the *real* message beneath their teen's behavior, not just to react to the nasty face value of the behavior. In many situations, your teen's anger is an attempt—sometimes intentional, but often not—to announce that certain core needs aren't being met, or are perceived as being unfairly denied, particularly by you.

For teens, anger tends to well up when they feel they're not getting:

Respect: Teens may flare during interactions with a parent because they assume their parent thinks they don't deserve respect. Teens often believe themselves to be more capable than their parents will admit.

S*pace*: Teens often want a parent to give them the physical and emotional room to try things out—to explore life without a parent's rules, reminders, and identity. Teens want their own identity.

V*alidation*: Teens generally experience things intensely. A teen's emotions are often strong and in flux. With all this intensity—and, believe it or not, because your perspective can have a great deal of impact—your teen sometimes looks to you for validation. Or, to use a less therapy-thick term, teens want to know a parent understands and accepts their feelings as real.

P*rovisions and Peers*: Teens also frequently want provisions or stuff from parents. This could be access to fun and distraction, this could be money. Provisions in this sense are primarily a route to connecting with peers. Teens generally want the acceptance and sense of belonging only peers can provide—and clothes and screens can seem like the keys to such experiences.

I'm sure none of these needs greatly surprises you. Perhaps you remember the importance of these when you were a teenager. Regardless, the mere knowledge of your teen's motivators isn't what will make the difference. Rather, it's your ability to communicate that you get it—that you realize, though you may not agree, that these things are very important to your teen. Communicating this will do much to create connection, and will serve as fuel to help improve your teen's behavior and capacity for managing the demands of daily life.

Remember: teens come by their anger honestly. Always. Your teen has no grand plan to screw with you. There's no early morning agenda that unfurls when a teen's eyes first open in the morning. While your teen certainly does things on purpose to irk, agitate, deflate, and deflect you, your teen doesn't plan to get mired in anger and suffering.

Ask Abblett

Q: So, are you saying my kid shouldn't be held accountable for his rants and destructive outbursts? That I should just let him off the hook because his anger problem is not his choice?

A: No, that's not what I'm saying. Yes, your teen does things on purpose—in the moment—to back you up or draw you in. But he doesn't intend for this cycle of suffering to repeat over and over. Still, he needs to be held accountable for actions that displace or hurt others. Accountability does not equate with complete culpability.

In *Acceptance and Commitment Therapy* (2011), psychologists Steven Hayes, Kirk Strosahl, and Kelly Wilson make the helpful distinction between *clean* and *dirty* emotions. Clean emotions are primary, basic reactions to stimulation from the environment. Clean emotions communicate a basic message that something is right or wrong for us. Clean anger occurs when someone directly and dangerously threatens your well-being, whether that's physically or psychologically. Here, anger, true to its primal roots, motivates us to take action to right our circumstances.

Dirty anger is different. Dirty anger is what our thoughts do in reaction to primary emotions. So, for example, dirty anger might cause us to assume accidental pain was caused by someone on purpose. We might become indignant and respond with, "How dare you!" Dirty anger is a layer of unnecessary mental muck we heap upon a primary emotion, be it anger, fear, or otherwise. It's a bit like taking one of the colors of a rainbow—the ROYGBIV you learned in middle school art class—and mixing it thoroughly with the others. You end up with a brownish, dirty mess.

We'll discuss why the human mind mixes up our emotional palette like this later. For now, know that our minds are constantly trying to protect us. Your mind registers emotions and makes snap judgments to help keep you out of harm's way. Problems occur when your system reacts out of proportion with the actual risks of a situation, or when you've been down a certain emotional road before and consequently now have a hair trigger for frustration.

This dirty anger is happening to you *and* to your teen. Teens' minds are trying to protect them as well. The whole system between you and your teen can become way out of sync—especially if deeper clinical factors are prompting your child's anger.

Mental Health Factors in Teen Anger

Sometimes a significant underlying clinical cause, such as depression, anxiety, or post-traumatic stress drives a teen's anger and acting out. To help your teen, it's important to consider—with professional input—whether your teen's anger goes beyond typical RSVP messages. Your teen's anger may derive from something that requires professional help.

In the 2010 National Comorbidity Survey, Dr. Kathleen Merikangas and colleagues interviewed over 10,000 American teens and found that about 32 percent met criteria for a diagnosable anxiety disorder at some point in their lives, 19 percent met criteria for a behavior disorder (such as oppositional defiant disorder), 14 percent for mood disorders (such as major depressive disorder), and about 11 percent for substance use disorders (Merikangas et al. 2010). Clearly, a large number of teens struggle with impairing emotional difficulties.

As a psychologist who has worked with at-risk, troubled youth for over fifteen years, I've heard a wide range of comments from parents grappling with the idea that there was some underlying clinical disorder driving their teen's anger. Here's a sampling:

"When he really gets going with an intense episode—when he's really losing it—I can't help but get terrified that this time he'll do it. This time he's really going to hurt himself or someone else."

"What do you mean she's sad? She sure doesn't act that way. To me, she's pissed off at the whole world."

"I have to walk on eggshells with him. If I don't help him sidestep things he doesn't want to deal with, then I become the target— I'm to blame."

"Sure, I know she's had a lot on her plate with our divorce and all. But I went through a lot of stuff too when I was her age, and I never dished it out to my parents and others in the family the way she does. There's no respect whatsoever."

"He has no friends. He's burned all his bridges."

Clinical conditions can manifest with significant angry behavior for adolescents, well beyond the RSVP reasons for anger. Though space does not allow for an exhaustive discussion of these conditions, I want to emphasize a few important points.

Anger Can Serve as a Mask for Depressed Mood in Teens

Anger can surface as a defensive crust for the overwhelming emotions and thoughts related to a depressive condition. I've noticed this with many boys I've helped and some girls as well. These teens may have extremely poor self-concepts. Some may feel so hopeless that they're actively considering suicide. They may not show much overt sadness, however, with the result that their depression can go undetected. This, in turn, can add to feelings of being unnoticed and unworthy, particularly by their family. Angry lashing out at loved ones, teachers, and other caregivers helps these teens feel a sense of control they have largely lacked. They typically don't believe themselves capable of having much positive impact in their lives—and don't expect good things to come their way. Anger becomes a predictable companion. They know what to expect with anger, even though it often leaves them with collateral damage at home, at school, and with peers.

Anger Can Give Teens a Way to Escape Intense Experiences of Anxiety

Stereotypically, we think of anxious kids as the wilting lilies of classrooms and gym class—the kids who shrink back, who work to keep out of the spotlight and below others' radar. And yet, some teens struggling with angry emotions and behavior may have a deep reservoir of fear lying just beneath their surliness. These teens are trying to avoid feeling deeply unsettling fears. If you block their escape routes— their preferred methods to duck and cover—you can end up experiencing the brunt of their anger. For example, some extremely anxious teens will attempt to opt out of school by feigning illness. If you, in responsible parent fashion, nudge them to go to school anyway— totally unaware of the cyberbullying from peers that's fueling their fear—you become the recipient of a tongue lashing. They make you out to be the worst parent ever, who yet again fails to fix things or understand what they're going through.

Anger Can Develop as a Self-Protective Mechanism When Teens Have Experienced Significant Loss or Trauma in Their Lives

When teens experience intense loss, physical or emotional abuse, or neglect, pain can lodge itself deep inside. Teens may be unable to sort through this pain alone. Perhaps a loved one has recently died, or they experienced trauma at the hands of someone they trusted, or a stranger took advantage of them. In cases like these, anger can become both the primary messenger, announcing that the psyche has been wounded, and the main method of defense against further injury. The underlying message is as follows: "If I lash out, I'll be able to keep people at a distance—I'll be able to keep them from hurting me again." It feels risky to show the hurt and fear resulting from these traumatic experiences, so instead they show anger. Parents are a safe dumping ground for teens' emotional pain. What a teen can't hold internally is temporarily managed by slinging it on to you.

You're likely well aware of the grief or trauma your teen has suffered—but your teen's anger can still be hard to face. While in quiet moments you may be able to compassionately connect with your teen, in moments of blazing anger such compassion can feel light years away.

Anger Can Be the Primary Clue that a Teen Has Suffered or Failed in Some Way in Relationships with Peers

Teens can be cruel. Teasing, slurs on Facebook, crushing your teen's reputation in the rumor mill—peers can be attacking your teen and you may be the last to learn of it. Perhaps your teen is engaged in a tit-for-tat, but that doesn't mean your teen deserves everything other teens are dishing out. You can end up the whipping-parent for your teen's peer-related pain. Your teen's anger can be a wake-up call that your teen needs your help. Remember, many teens spend much of their waking life thinking about and obsessing over how they stand with their peers. When peer relationships go poorly—when your teen has been maligned or rejected—it can fuel anger.

Deciding If It's Time for Professional Help

If your teen's anger appears to be a clear reaction to a neglected RSVP—that is, if your teen appears to feel disrespected, intruded upon, emotionally invalidated, or blocked from tangible stuff the teen wants—then you may be able to manage things on your own. If, however, your teen's anger is long-standing, highly disruptive to daily self-management, toxic to the functioning of your household, or is escalating into severe episodes of aggression, depression, or risk-taking behavior (such as unprotected sex or substance abuse), then professional intervention is crucial. While it is never easy emotionally to reach out to professionals—and can be expensive, inconvenient, stig-matizing, and anything but a sure thing—in these cases the risks of going it alone are too great.

Professionals experienced in working with adolescents have knowl-edge, training, and the perspective you lack by nature of being a parent. While professionals aren't perfect and may disagree with one another, they can provide the lifeline families need in clinically significant situ-ations with teens. This book is a resource, but it is not a living, breath-ing guide who can address the specifics of what's happening in your family.

It Takes Two to Get Tangled in Anger

We've surveyed some of the core factors that create anger problems for teens. Now let's turn to solutions. This book focuses primarily not on your teen's problem behavior, but on improving the communication between you and your teen.

A more connected relationship *is* possible even when things have been toxic between you and your teen. The remainder of this book will help you maximize the chances for creating this connection.

All parents of teens who are struggling need a heaping dose of hope that things can change for the better. They can. This book, however, isn't about the future. Rather, it's about what you're commu-nicating to your teen in the present moment. What you'll find is that, as communication improves, your teen's problem behaviors generally improve as well. Building communication and relationship skills between parent and teen can go a long way to addressing both the now and the long term.

As a family therapist, I once worked with a single mom and her fourteen-year-old son. Despite having a great deal of intellectual ability, this teen had struggled in school for years. The teen's primary obstacles were an angry, irritable mood and attention difficulties; these dis-rupted his ability to focus as well as to feel competent socially and academically. After weeks of escalating behavior at home (and refusals to leave for school) morphed into months, the mom was desperate.

Amid pained looks out the office window, she told me, "He's going to ruin his life if he keeps this up... No one gets what's going on here—not even people in my own family. They either just blame me, blame him, or both of us... I end up doing one of two things: I either give him anything he wants to get him out of bed and onto the bus—chocolate for breakfast, even the gift card I had in my purse—or I end up screaming and threatening to send him away to one of those wilderness programs."

Crying, she added, "He's so damn smart and yet he's failing at school. Sometimes I'm convinced he's just conning me, doing all this shit on purpose to get what he wants. Maybe I'm just a damn fool."

When son and mother sat together in my office, their postures aimed away from each other as if they were battling magnetic poles, each shoving the other away. The back and forth continued:

"I'm done with that school. It's full of retards and I'm not going."

"You need to watch your language."

"Why? I don't give a shit," the son said. "You think I'm too stupid to cut it in college anyway, so what's the use?"

"There he goes with the disrespect again. It never stops!"

"Just back off me, or I'll make you wish you had! I know your boyfriend has about had it with you because of me, so don't think I won't make it a little more likely he leaves."

"See, Doc? There's no helping this kid," the mother said. "Maybe you can talk some sense into him."

There was a time in my work as a clinician focused on adolescents and their parents that I would have talked to this family about the tug-of-war going on between them. I would have focused on the issues of power and control that led to these outbursts. I would have worked to give them strategies to meet their control needs in other ways.

However, over the years I've found that although this approach could be helpful at times, it was only helpful to a point. It missed something. It treated the tug-of-war between parent and teen as if it were a bad thing, a problem to be dropped. What I've learned—and what research increasingly supports—is that when teens and parents struggle most, this tug-of-war needs a different sort of attention. Instead of dropping the tug-of-war rope, parent and teen need to hold on. They need to learn how to keep themselves tethered to one another in healthy ways that get their respective needs met.

This particular boy needed medication and other therapeutic interventions to address underlying attention and emotional issues. However, the relationship between mother and son needed addressing as well—and the problem was not the rope, it was *how* they were holding it. What they needed was a new way of communicating.

The Anatomy of Parent–Teen Communication

Over millennia, the human brain evolved in response to demands to communicate with others in our species (Wilson 2004). Humans weren't the fastest, strongest, or even toothiest species around, yet we came to dominate the planet due to our capacities for symbolizing experience through language. With thoughts and images, humans were able to both represent experiences internally and develop the physical and psychological capacities to express these to one another.

The interconnected structures our brains evolved not only help us communicate, they also help us develop emotional "ropes" that tether us together. (Psychologists call this *attachment*.) Together, language and attachment shape the drama—the highs and lows—of relationships.

You cannot *not* communicate. Think about it: you cannot look someone in the eyes without, in at least some very small nuanced way, sending the person a message. Try it. Sit or stand facing someone—stranger, friend, family member, it doesn't matter. Set a timer for thirty seconds and then look each other in the eyes. Try very hard not to communicate anything to the other person.

You will fail. As have the hundreds of people I've done this exercise with, you will inevitably send some sort of message. Why? As biologists increasingly argue, our brains are wired for communication (Goleman 2007; Seigel and Hartzell 2004). We evolved as communication gurus. Anger is part of this cerebral hardware. Our capacity to flare at one another helped us survive in harsh, prehistoric environments when predators came our way.

We do not, however, live in caves anymore (though the unkempt state of your teen's room might suggest otherwise), and we do not have saber-toothed tigers breathing down our necks. While the modern world certainly holds dangers, relative to our ancestors' world, today we live in daily safety.

And yet, we continue to have the same biology—including the parts of our brains involved in experiencing and expressing anger. We all trip over our brain's wiring when sending messages to loved ones, because we all still have brains designed to scan our environments for danger and jump to the conclusions necessary to keep us alive. Further, our brain's attachment system ties us together with strong emotions, flooding us with anger, resentment, fear, and (insert any other negative emotion here). Our brains were not built for the modern age of nuance, mixed messages, and family complexities, where inner calm in the face of threat is much more advantageous than is an angry swipe of the fist.

Again, we all trip over the three-pound relics in our skulls. There's no blame in that. There is, though, responsibility. As the parent, the messages you send will set the tone for communication with your teen. Remember, you cannot not communicate. So, setting aside the constraints of your brain's architecture, what messages do you want to send?

As you'll experience when you engage in the activities and practices of this book, you can change your brain's wiring. The science is increasingly clear (Lazar et al. 2000; Vestergaard-Poulsen et al. 2009): the brain physically changes in response to many of the strategies I describe here. Consequently, you *can* alter your patterns of communication— and new, healing messages *can* get through to your teen.

And from you, your teen can learn to send such messages as well.

What Makes a Communication Breakdown?

A communication breakdown begins in the microseconds when our mirror neurons—specialized brain cells that react to emotions and actions of others—fire faster than our thoughts and intentions can keep up. Thinking, taking perspective, and feeling compassion in response to someone's behavior happens in the cerebral cortex, an evolutionarily more recent place of the brain.

When we observe someone doing something emotional, our mirror neurons spark the older, emotional centers of the brain to process this information before our cerebral cortex does or can. As a result, we see our teen's emotion—and begin reacting intensely ourselves—much more quickly than our cortex can produce grounded, compassionate thoughts. Our cortex stumbles along, trying to keep pace with the emotional brain. The fact that this happens behind both sets of eyeballs yields the breakdown—your and your teen's poor frontal lobes barely stand a chance!

If you tried the eye contact exercise described previously—and if you haven't yet, I recommend trying it with someone now—you will have discovered that you quickly failed because you couldn't help communicating in some way. When you locked eyes with the other person, your respective brains were on fire with activity, priming reactions to what you were seeing. When that other person is your own child, particularly one with whom emotions and messages have been challenging, communication easily gets sidetracked.

Remember, struggling teens do the aggressive, antagonistic, disruptive, and sometimes downright dangerous things they do in order to send messages. They are looking for you to RSVP—to give them the respect, space, validation, and provisions for connecting to peers they feel are lacking or threatened.

Research suggests that parents whose communication with their teens is filled with conflict messages are more likely to disengage—that is, inadequately communicate; such disengaging contributes to less parental monitoring and greater risk for behavioral or substance abuse difficulties among young people (Dishion, Nelson, and Bullock

2004). Again, communication breakdowns aren't just about a loss of control, they're complicated at a brain-to-brain level. Communication breakdowns are about the nuances of rapidly processing information in the brain combined with a lack of methods for initiating real, loving messages between parent and teen.

Here's a more hopeful finding: parent–teen relationships marked by closeness, open communication, and reduced conflict have been shown to facilitate teens' development of self-regulation skills, emotional well-being, and positive social behaviors (Masten and Coatsworth 1998).

Let me emphasize, there are no June Cleaver–shaped genes for good parenting. It's not that some people are born expert at managing challenges with teens. However, communication skills based in mindfulness and positive approaches can actually change the physical structure of the brain and make helping your teen much easier.

The Destructive Dance Between Parents and Teens

This may seem surprising, but parents and teens also mutually teach each other to escalate things. As with what's happening at a biological level in the brain, this learning—called operant conditioning—happens without anyone choosing it. It's largely unintentional and no one's really to blame. That said, you can learn to recognize and interrupt this pattern with the tools presented in this book.

Gerald Patterson (1982) and colleagues at the University of Oregon coined the term *parent–child coercive cycle* to describe the pattern in which parent and child mutually influence each other in subtle ways to increase the stuck quality of their interactions and erode communication. Studies ranging over thirty years link these cycles to increased risk of behavioral problems in youth (Granic and Patterson 2006).

Consider this example: a seventeen-year-old named Jason sprawls on his bed, his fingers flying across his smartphone as he texts his friends. Dirty laundry is strewn about the room, all in the exact same spots where he'd peeled the clothes off, in some cases two weeks prior. His father enters the room and is struck by the stale smell.

"I thought I told you to put all this laundry in the hamper. Is it too much to ask for you to listen to me for once?!"

Jason doesn't say anything, but shakes his head and makes mimicking mouth movements while he continues to tap away at his phone.

"So you're going to just ignore me again? Is that the deal?" the father yells. "I've had it with you, Jason. You have no respect for me or for yourself by tossing your nasty clothes around like this."

Jason looks up from his phone and glares. "Get the fuck out of my room! I've had it with you, too. You have no fucking clue what respect means anyway!"

The father walks to a pair of jeans, picks them up, and angrily throws them into the hamper. "Wow! You're right, that's such a chore!" he yells and walks out of the room.

Jason flips the middle finger at his father's back and returns to texting, shaking his head with an indignant expression on his face.

How familiar is this example for you? In this instance, the parent initiated the sequence by presenting a demand (to pick up dirty laundry). But the teen can also be the one who presents a request or demand that sparks this cycle (see figures 1.1 and 1.2 below for a breakdown of the cycle in both situations). In coercive cycles like this one, parent and teen both punish and reinforce each other. *Punish* and *reinforce* are technical terms in psychology that describe how responses to behavior either make a behavior more likely in the future by being rewarding (reinforcement) or less likely by being aversive (punishment).

What's happening here is a process of mutual triggering. The teen's anger increases, punishing the parent. This continues until the parent's demand, which is aversive and punishing for the teen, is either removed or the parent gives the teen what the teen wants. If the parent drops the subject, this reinforces and thereby increases the teen's angry behavior. If the parent gives the teen what the teen wants, this reinforces the parent's giving-in behavior, making it more likely in the future.

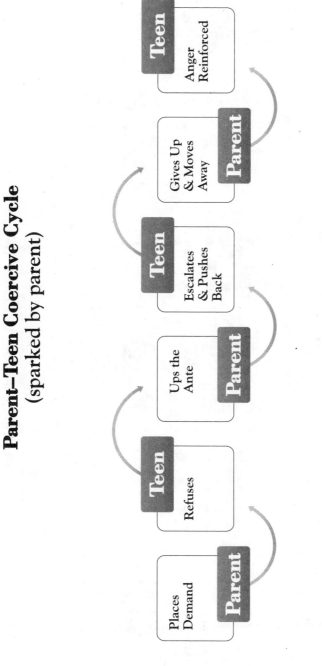

Figure 1.1: Parent–Teen Coercive Cycle (sparked by parent)

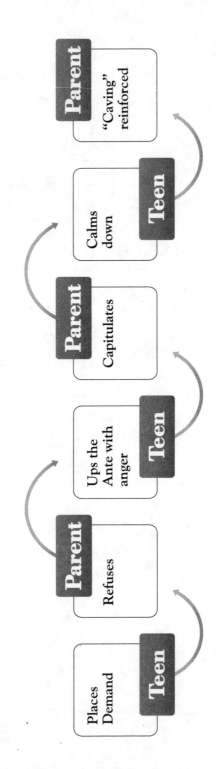

Parent–Teen Coercive Cycle
(sparked by teen)

Figure 1.2: Parent–Teen Coercive Cycle (sparked by teen)

As a result of all this mutual punishing and reinforcing, cycles can feel hopelessly deadlocked. Communication breaks down as both parents' and teens' valid perspectives and needs are lost in the shuffle. In the example above, the parent has a valid need for cleanliness in the family home, as well as respect from his child. The teen has a valid need for his own space, into which his parent can't intrude at will. Neither is able to appreciate the other's needs.

With each repetition of the cycle, resentment, pain, anger, and the cycle itself solidify further. What you need are tools to interrupt these cycles and slow down the activity in the brain. This will give you—and your teen—a chance to sidestep anger, to start communicating directly, and to connect. It's here that the PURE method (presented below), with its focus on mindfulness and positive psychology skills, can help.

What Is Mindfulness and How Does It Help?

The word mindfulness gets tossed about a lot these days, but what exactly *is* mindfulness? Let's start by defining what mindfulness is *not*:

- Mindfulness does not require sitting on special cushions, wearing maroon robes, or going on retreats.

- Mindfulness may feel spiritual, but it doesn't have to be.

- Mindfulness doesn't mean becoming passive or a pushover. You can be very active, direct, and assertive *and* be mindful.

- Mindfulness is definitely not numbing or shutting off your thoughts and feelings. Rather, mindfulness involves actually staying very much in contact with what's happening, but in a more flexible way. This is crucial for building better communication with your teen.

Noted mindfulness author and teacher Jon Kabat-Zinn defines mindfulness as "the awareness that arises by paying attention on purpose in the present moment and non-judgmentally." (2013: xxxv)

That's it. Sounds simple, right? It is. It's also an extremely difficult way to consistently live.

But You Already Know Mindfulness

Mindfulness is not new to you, even in your parenting of this now-teenager. You were perhaps mindful when your child was born, or, if adopted, first came into your arms. You may have been mindful when beholding an amazing sunset, or when you met the eyes of a loved one after a gift that left you breathless, or when you felt the basketball in your hand and nothing else. What *is* new is your willingness to cultivate mindfulness as a set of skills for communicating effectively with your teen. Your intention toward greater and greater mindfulness in your relationship *will* lead to changes.

A growing body of research links mindfulness skills in parenting to positive outcomes in the relationship between parent and child. In one study, a mindfulness-based family intervention was shown to improve family functioning and reduce the potential for child abuse in comparison to a control condition (Dawe and Harnett 2007). A randomized trial with early adolescent youth that tested a mindful parenting program demonstrated improved child behavior outcomes, as well as improved parent–youth relationship qualities (Duncan, Coatsworth, and Greenberg 2009).

The research is clear: when adults and kids learn to become present with their senses and thoughts—to practice mindfulness—the negative effects of stress on health decrease; attention and concentration improve; ruminative thinking, low moods, and anxiety decrease; and well-being rises (Brown and Ryan 2003). Isn't that motivation enough to start digging into these skills with your teen?

Ask Abblett

Q: So is the take-home message that I need to become a Buddhist and things will improve with my daughter?

A: Mindfulness is certainly at the center of Buddhism, as it is for Hinduism and Taoism—and, for that matter, many athletic endeavors. Mindfulness is not about religion or any form of worship. Mindfulness is about building a reverence for the present moment, about becoming aware of what is, and doing so with flexibility and nonjudgment. Mindfulness will bring you out of rigid thinking and unhelpful reflexive reactions to help you forge new pathways of connection with your daughter.

So how does mindfulness work to help you parent your teen? Well, in three ways:

1. Mindfulness helps you stay in the present moment. By keeping your attention centered on a chosen object (such as your breath) and bringing it back to that object when distracted, you build the muscle of concentration in your brain. This trains your mind to stay in the present moment, rather like training a dog to stay.

2. Mindfulness gives you insight into your own thought patterns. By noticing and labeling where your mind goes during mindfulness practice, you start to know your mind better, to learn its triggers, patterns, and habits. These insights help you prepare for situations that can trigger an avalanche of reactions when communicating with your teen.

3. Mindfulness helps you be less judgmental. By being gentle and kind to yourself when your mind wanders off during mindfulness practice, you create a new habit of being compassionate with yourself. Being compassionate with ourselves is not something most of us are in the habit of doing, especially when things are stressful and going awry with our children.

Throughout this book, you'll learn how to be more mindful of the things you see, touch, hear, taste, and smell, as well as of the words and images you hold in your mind. We'll practice skills that not only build mindfulness to make interactions more fun and enjoyable, but also help you to connect with what's really happening for your teen, inside and out.

Most people, most of the time—especially when angry—focus on stressful events from the past or future stressors on the horizon. This is particularly true for parents with regard to their children. Such mental time travel away from the present is a big part of what causes us to suffer. A wise supervisor once told me that all our suffering boils down to one statement we buy into without hesitation: "It shouldn't be this way." It's on adults to help teens learn to get out of their heads and into what's actually going on—to learn how to ride out the challenges and embrace what's awesome.

In many ways, mindfulness is embedded within the idea of presence. And when you put all of your awareness and attention on what's happening right now in your experience of your senses, healthy choices and actions become more likely. Presence is thus the first step toward addressing the communication breakdown with your teen.

Are you willing to learn to harness the power of the present moments of your relationship with your teen? In the end, these moments are all we have. The stories we tell ourselves—our imagined narratives of past and future—pale in comparison to what we have when we claim moments in mindfulness. How about claiming them with your child?

What Positive Psychology Brings to the Table

In addition to mindfulness, this book introduces you to what the science of positive psychology has to offer your relationship with your struggling teenager.

When I first heard the term positive psychology toward the end of my training years, it conjured up searches for rainbows and unicorns. This new happy-focused branch of my field seemed a little light on substance and a little heavy on affirmations.

I was wrong. Positive psychology, or the study of the *how* of happiness, is hard science, and it has shown that we've been approaching some things backwards for a long time. When it comes to happiness, we've been conditioned to think we must do, be, and acquire many things to demonstrate we're successful, and *then* we'll be happy. What research in positive psychology shows is the reverse: that when we do, be, and acquire happiness-related thoughts, feelings, and actions, success tends to follow (Seligman 2002; Achor 2010).

Positive psychology studies how we can generate perspective, inner (emotional and cognitive) and outer (behavioral) flexibility, and excellence in our daily pursuits. Positive psychology is about finding flow in our work and relationships (Csikszentmihalyi 1998) and developing a growth mindset for facing life's challenges (Dweck 2006). It's about consciously cultivating your social support network (Uchino 2004) and spreading goodwill to others in a way that amps up your own well-being and effectiveness (Biswas-Diener, Kashdan, and Minhas 2011). Positive psychology teaches us to guide our mindset, emotions, and behavior in order to build life satisfaction ourselves instead of waiting around and hoping that the bluebird of happiness will magically land on our heads. Positive psychology's practices are powerful antidotes to the toxic experience of unchecked anger.

That's why I've built mindfulness and positive psychology into this book. These practices help get at what's hardest about managing things with your teen—and they do so without increasing worry or pessimism or labeling your teen as conduct disordered. While it's important not to bury our heads in the sand about disruptive and debilitating conditions, it's also not helpful to anyone to have diagnoses, syndromes, and disease entities be the sole focus of the field dedicating itself to improving the mental and emotional circumstances of an entire society. One of the primary skills from positive psychology you'll practice is shifting your frame for understanding your teen's behavior.

Findings from positive psychology include:

- Developing self-control in one area of your life leads to greater self-control in others (Baumeister and Tierney 2012).

- Creating a daily habit of tracking reasons for being grateful leads to increased optimism and effectiveness in performance situations (Achor 2010).

- Inventing positive *counterfacts*, or a positive explanatory style, after a difficult experience leads to increased ability to successfully cope with challenges (Seligman 2006).

- Playing to one's strengths significantly increases well-being and performance at work (Linley 2008).

These findings are just a brief sample. Throughout the book we'll explore how perspectives and skills that draw on positive psychology can improve your situation with your teen.

Now let's turn to the key underlying structure of this book: the PURE method of communication.

The PURE Method of Dealing with Communication Breakdowns

The PURE method of communication is built around a set of skills that, taken together, can help you break the stalemate between you and your angry teen and allow you to parent with a lot less conflict:

Presence or a mindfulness of sense experience

Understanding or a mindfulness of thoughts paired with compassionate perspective-taking

Responsive leadership or leading interactions forward with clear, consistent communication

Empowerment or affirming autonomy and choice regardless of the situation

Figure 1.3 shows our roadmap for this book. The PURE method is best thought of as a series of steps that represent the ideal responses for parents when teens are struggling.

While this sequence of communication moves is ideal, it is not an immediate cure for all of the problems occurring in your relationship with your teen. If you're reading this book, things have likely built into a "toxic" or stuck state over time. It will take time to "purify" the communication, to enhance the relationship and reduce the problems for your teen. A filter doesn't immediately transform sewage into pure drinking water. Sewage water needs to flow through the filter for some time before it becomes purified.

The PURE Communication Intervention Method©

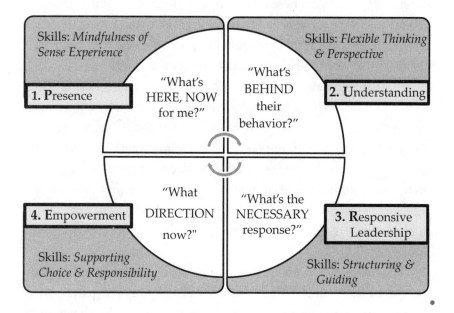

Figure 1.3: The PURE Communication Intervention Method

A core principle of the PURE method of communication is that parents must practice presence at the start of any challenging parenting situation. Again, presence here is a mindfulness of sensation and emotion that allows for balanced, flexible responses. Even if a parent merely takes a short mindful pause, the parent's next action to communicate with an angry teen will be much more likely to be effective.

We'll spend the next chapter learning and practicing such skills of presence so that you can nonjudgmentally hold the experience rather than react in kneejerk fashion. Not only must a parent start with presence, the parent must carry mindfulness forward through the rest of the interaction.

Once firmly established in present-moment awareness, the parent can then turn to the second step: seeking to understand what lies behind the teen's angry and disruptive behavior. This requires sidestepping biased, rigid thinking. What is it that's most real for your teen that makes these actions so urgent? That's perhaps protecting the teen in some way? The goal here is for parents to learn the habit of curiosity about the inner experience of their teen. By communicating this curiosity, parents show that they are willing to hold not only their own reactions, but want to help teens hold their own as well.

After understanding comes a crossroads moment. This is when your teen is expecting a lecture, reprimand, or perhaps a cold shoulder from you. Your teen may also be expecting confusion, distress, or downright despair. With responsive leadership, parents learn to do and show the opposite. Instead of moving too forcefully in or pulling too far away, parents mindfully lean in and lead the teen with support, structure, and guidance. Again, parents move to this third step of the PURE method with presence and understanding already tucked under their arms.

The interaction—and an entire interaction may take only twenty seconds or less—ends with an empowerment move. The parent offers a supportive reminder that the teen gets to choose what happens in their own mind and behavior, and that a parent can't dictate those things. The parent speaks from the heart and lets the teen know what truly matters, including that the parent notices even the smallest positive efforts. At this point, parents should also quietly give themselves kudos for doing all they can to communicate their loving, supportive intentions despite a difficult interaction.

It's the rare teen who at this point suddenly looks up, anger melting with peaceful relief, and says: "Why thank you, Mom or Dad! I appreciate you validating my feelings and giving me support and guidance despite my ranting and swearing! Very kind of you!" (You'd probably spontaneously combust in disbelief if your teen did this anyway.)

What does happen, though, is that after multiple PURE cycles your teen will begin to trust that a different pattern of communication with you is not only possible, it's already happening. Things will feel better. The overall energy will shift toward solutions and connection and away from breakdown and lashing out.

Let's return to the example from my practice of the fourteen-year-old and his mom. In the moment after the boy threatens to trigger a breakup between his mom and her boyfriend, the mom could choose to try a PURE communication cycle.

> **P**resence: The mom breathes in, fully notices the sensations in her body, and gently labels them with the thought, *Anger is here.* She breathes into these sensations and notices space around them.

> **U**nderstanding: The mom notices that she is *having the thought* to tell him he's a little ass and is going to spend the summer in a residential program if he doesn't cut it out. She looks up at her son, his face warped with disgust, and she looks past the disgust for another breath's worth of pausing. She wonders about the pain there for him. The pain they've not talked about in months. She talks slowly and with a lightness in her face as she looks at him. "I really have underestimated how hard it's been for you with me dating Dan these past few months. I can see how it would feel easier if he weren't around to complicate things and pull my attention away from you."

> **R**esponsive Leadership: The teen rolls his eyes, but does not lash out again. His anger seems to have stalled. The mom leans in toward her son, her voice somehow softer and yet more urgent. "I want to quit missing what's important for you. It's on me that I haven't been there to really listen, and I'm sorry for that. It's important for us to respect each other. I need to listen *and* I

need you to work on talking more respectfully to me. I'm hoping we can work on this together."

Empowerment: The boy looks at his mom. Disbelief and mistrust are stamped on his face. "Yeah right," he mutters. The mom breathes again, maintaining presence and reconnecting with the understanding of what's behind his behavior. "It's up to you if you want to work on your piece, just as much as it's up to me to be responsible for mine. I'm up for it if you are. Actually, I'm up for it even if you're not ready to. I can't make you choose."

Yes, this is an ideal set of PURE responses from the mother. And yes, though you will stumble many times (I still do!), this sort of communication is possible for you. As we'll see, it's not about being a tree-hugging pacifist in the face of threats and risky behavior from your teen. You will set limits on your teen's behavior, but you'll do so with much greater internal and external flexibility. You'll have more options open to you, and your teen will be much more likely to experience you as compassionate and caring.

Now, let's get on the path of practice.

Basics of Mindfulness

When we practice mindfulness, whether for a few seconds or longer, we simply rest our mind on something in the present moment. We can do this either by concentrating on a specific anchor, such as the sensations of our breathing, or by noticing whatever is happening in our senses with full, nonjudgmental attention from moment to moment—what we can call *open awareness*. Whether through concentration or open awareness, mindfulness helps us realize how our minds habitually race to the past or future, while our bodies and five senses exist only here in the present. When our mind wanders, we notice where it has gone, and our mindfulness skills gently bring our mind back to experiencing the here and now. Again, notice that mindfulness involves three parts: intentional attention, being present in the moment, and acceptance/nonjudgment. "Presence," as I use it in the PURE method, is mindfulness of what's showing up in one's physical senses in a given moment.

Throughout the book, we'll explore various activities to help you develop mindful presence. Remember, mindfulness skills are a crucial first step to transforming communication breakdowns with your teen. Without this foundation, little else will work, and breakdowns will continue.

Let's begin with a couple of quick activities that demonstrate the power of presence. They are also excellent tools for grounding yourself in the here and now. I recommend returning to them frequently.

Skill Practice: Sounds Around

1. Wherever you are, pause what you're doing.

2. Take a slow breath in and out through the nose.

3. Gently close your eyes.

4. Start to notice the sounds arising around you, beginning with those nearby and extending to the more subtle sounds in the distance.

5. Without judging or analyzing the sounds, collect the sounds as they come, silently counting them with your fingers.

6. If you become distracted by thoughts, gently return to collecting the sounds around you.

7. Once you've collected a sound for each of your fingers, open your eyes.

Notice that the sounds came to you, that you didn't have to search with your attention to find them. How might you allow the sounds of your relationship with your teen to come to you, rather than going out in search of the next conversation or argument?

A key aspect of mindfulness is trusting your awareness of what is in the moment over what your thoughts yell at you to do or say—or not do or not say. Of course, you need to think when you're interacting with your teen. As you build mindfulness skills, you'll begin to notice whether all this thinking really helps you to help your teen. Have you been able to think your way into a connected relationship with your teen?

Let's try a mindfulness practice focused on sensations of breath and body movement.

Skill Practice: Whiffs of Wakefulness

This is a great activity for developing awareness of your breathing, waking yourself up, and relaxing your entire body. Pure heaven for the tapped-out parent of a teen!

1. Stand with your feet shoulder-width apart. Feel your feet grounded on the floor; feel a strong sense of being rooted there, as if your feet were growing deep into the earth below.

2. With eyes open, begin to inhale slowly and deeply through the nose. As you do, gently raise both hands back and out to the sides, as if you're embracing the sky. Gently arch backward, so that you're looking upward.

3. Exhale slowly from the mouth. As you do, slowly fold yourself forward and down. Imagine that your body is a bellows and you are slowly squeezing all the air from your lungs. Continue to fold forward until your arms dangle down toward your feet and all your breath has been expelled.

4. Repeat the process: inhale, arching your back and opening your arms out, then exhale, folding in and bending down.

5. Continue for several cycles.

6. Stand upright, your hands loose at your sides. Close your eyes. Notice how your body feels. Notice any tingling, any energy moving in your body. Notice how your mind has shifted during this practice.

Basics of Positive Psychology

Now let's start building the positive infrastructure that will help shift your communication with your teen. Here are two short practices that will help you cultivate clarity and change in your parenting.

Skill Practice: Parental Power Questions

Research is clear: our perspective on events—our mindset or frame for what's happening—is crucial to the sorts of outcomes we experience. A study by Stanford University psychologist Carol Dweck (2006), on growth or flexible mindsets versus fixed or rigid mindsets, found that children and adults who adopt a growth mindset fare much better with regard to grades, productivity, and the like than those who adopt a fixed mindset.

In this practice, you'll apply a growth perspective to your parenting. Remember, even though things may have seemed stuck for some time, that can be changed.

1. Consider a recent communication with your teen that seemed to hit a dead end.

2. Finish the following sentence: "When it comes to addressing this situation I _____."

3. If you finished the sentence with anything like, "have thrown up my hands," or, "have tried everything and don't have a clue what to try next," or, "think it's really my kid's fault," then try the following:

4. With your eyes closed, visualize your teen's appearance and behavior during the communication breakdown. Set aside any rigid mental chatter and consider the following power questions:

    What am I willing to give my teen right now so that my teen sees how much I want to help us out of this situation?

    What's more important to do in the next moment: venting and reacting, or doing and saying what matters most?

    What am I willing to risk in myself in order for my teen to see how much I care about connecting?

5. Imagine what might happen next if you acted from one of these internal power questions. Would it be the same breakdown as usual, or might there be some space for growth?

Let's wind down now with a core practice to build your overall skills in mindfulness and positive self-management.

Peaceful Parent Practice: WHEN Is My Mind?

This practice focuses on what I refer to as offline skills. These skills, spread throughout the book, are offline in the sense that they are meant to be practiced when you have the time and space to do so, not in the moment when things are difficult with your teen. These core practices lay a foundation that supports your own well-being and helps you hang in there. Think of offline practice as similar to going to the gym to get fit—you have to keep showing up to achieve the results you want.

In a quiet space, take a few minutes to practice the following:

1. Sit in an upright, alert posture with your eyes closed.

2. Settle in. Take a couple of deep, centering breaths.

3. Step into a timeless machine. This is the opposite of a time machine. The timeless machine doesn't move you backward or forward in time; it erases time altogether—there's only the present moment.

4. Consider: When, as a parent, have you experienced a sense of time falling away? When have you been so engaged, focused, and aware that you became lost in whatever it was you were doing?

5. Don't analyze or judge whatever emerges. Just notice and experience it, no matter how mundane or magnificent it may seem.

6. Take another deep, full breath. Quietly continue to notice your thoughts and feelings about this activity.

The timeless machine shows you what you do—or have done—as a parent that is so engaging that you lose track of time. These are the activities and interactions that you just flow into. Once you're doing them, things groove and thoughts go quiet. Even if you're exhausted by your teen's anger these days, consider: what are the timeless things you do with your teen, or for your teen, that you don't have to be convinced to do?

For me, one of these timeless things is making a silly duck voice so that my toddler Theo giggles uncontrollably. Another is having car chats with my kindergartener Celia. In one recent car chat Celia informed me that "the other cars can't hear you yelling—they'll move out of our way on their own." (Who's teaching mindfulness to whom?)

The point here is to pause amidst all the stress and remember that connection is most likely to happen when past and future drop away and there's only the now of sharing. These timeless moments are what parenting should be about.

Practice noticing these moments—sometimes small, sometimes large. Don't let them mindlessly slide past your awareness. Note them, be *in* them. Savor their sights and sounds. Record the experiences—jot them down in a journal, the margin of this book, somewhere. When you're with your teen, practice noticing these timeless moments on a regular basis. You'll be astounded by what you would have otherwise missed.

These moments can become the basis for you to connect in a more authentic way with your teen. This practice of noticing can break you free of blinders and help you see possibilities for positive change.

And here's what's really great: most teens will notice *you* noticing *them*. When you practice this strategy you send a powerful message of curiosity and openness. Both are important in establishing new patterns of communication and connection with your teen.

Your Parental Agenda

Before you move on to the next chapter:

- ☐ Review the RSVP needs that typically underlie anger in teens. Explore in your journal how these might be relevant for your teen.

- ☐ Consider the clinical factors that can contribute to anger; investigate consulting a licensed mental health professional, particularly one specializing in clinical work with adolescents.

- ☐ Try to identify coercive cycles that may be operating between you and your teen. How may practicing the PURE method of communication benefit your situation?

- ☐ Journal honestly about your intentions in working through this book. Are you merely looking to get your child to behave, or are you willing to work on the overall health of your relationship?

- ☐ Practice the mindfulness and positive psychology exercises with an attitude of patience and openness.

2 Presence: Mindfulness of the Senses for Managing Heat from Teens

These days you can't pass a magazine rack without seeing something about the power of mindfulness. We're bombarded by news about mindfulness—that it helps reduce the effects of stress, that it improves immune function and even decision-making skills. In this chapter, we delve into how it can play a helpful, healing role in your parenting.

In this chapter you will:

- Take a brief self-assessment to help target your mindfulness-development needs.

- Learn and practice mindfulness techniques that create stability, clarity, resilience, and openness, even when parenting a teen struggling with anger.

Mindfulness: The Oxygen of Effective Parenting

Controlled scientific studies overwhelmingly establish mindfulness as valuable for living a healthy, engaged, less stressful life (Hoffman et al. 2010; Grossman et al. 2004). As discussed in chapter 1, mindfulness has been shown to change the structure of the brain in measurable and meaningful ways (Vestergaard-Poulsen et al. 2009).

And yet, the promise of mindfulness can seem far out of reach. Practicing mindfulness seems to take much more time than modern life allows. The bar seems too high for the non–Dalai Lamas among us to attain. For the parent of an angry teen, mindfulness can feel simply unmanageable. It's not. You're likely practicing mindfulness right now. The act of bringing your attention to bear on the words and ideas presented here, with an open, curious attitude, makes you as enlightened in this moment as a seasoned mediator.

Think of mindfulness as oxygen. When you're mindful, you attend fully to what's happening in the present moment. This attention to the *now* nourishes your mind and body, just like oxygen nourishes living things. Mindfulness helps people make good choices, relax, and enjoy things more. And, like a fresh breeze, mindfulness also blows away the dust coating our emotions and thoughts, bringing clarity to what previously was obscured.

This book teaches you how to be more mindful with your senses—as you see, touch, hear, taste, and smell—in order to heighten your capacity to manage your teen's anger. Mindfulness helps cool the emotional heat of anger and rigid thinking. Just as a fresh breeze tempers the heat of a summer day, maintaining a mindful awareness of your sense experiences can help you manage the heat of the moment with your teen.

Mindful Parenting Self-Assessment

Take a moment to ask yourself the following questions about your situation with your teen:

1. Do you frequently feel flooded or overwhelmed by the physical sensations of emotions when trying to manage communication with your teen?

2. Is the stress of interacting with your teen building up in your body, wearing you down, and sapping your resilience?

3. Are you often inundated by distracting thoughts and emotions about your teen, to the point that you can't seem to keep yourself centered?

4. Do you struggle with the emotional effects of rigid thinking, either directed toward your teen or yourself?

5. Does it feel as if the situation will always be stuck?

6. Do you find yourself gritting your teeth in response to your frustration, trying to somehow push it all away?

Perhaps you answered yes to only one of the above questions. Perhaps you answered yes to all six. Don't get lost in how many yes responses you had. Instead, simply notice yourself having any negative reactions—without judgment.

Each question points to a challenge that mindfulness skills can address. This chapter teaches you specific practices for doing so. The following matching mindfulness targets can help you identify where to focus going forward:

1. *Anchoring*: becoming grounded in your present-moment sense experience.

2. *Body awareness*: soothing the stress that builds up in the body.

3. *Focus*: becoming centered when difficult situations are disorganized and distracting.

4. *Flexible thinking*: creating a more effective, looser relationship to your own thinking so that it doesn't bind you.

5. *Widened perspective*: opening your sense of present—and future—and moving away from tunnel vision shaped by the pain of the past.

6. *Acceptance*: developing the capacity to ride out pain once it's arrived on the scene.

How Mindfulness Soothes Tough Interactions with Teens

When you practice skills of mindful presence—the first of the four steps of the PURE method—you choose to shift your attention away from what your reactive mind is screaming at you and toward what is actually happening inside your body. Mindful presence takes you out of the unhelpful content of emotional thoughts and into the observation of bodily sensations as they are, without labels or judgments. Presence gives you space and flexibility, making situations less overwhelming.

When your teen is glaring at you as you clash about curfew yet again, mindfulness skills bring you out of the reactive mental chatter, and into the felt sensations of your body. Mindfulness deliteralizes what's happening inside you. Mindfulness makes things less red-hot urgent, though the situation may be extremely challenging. Presence creates a strong yet adaptable foundation for parenting in the heat of the moment. Even in potentially dangerous situations, flexible action is better than reactive flailing.

Consider: when are you more likely to be able to take effective action, when you're frantically trying to control painful feelings, or when you hold yourself calmly despite an unpleasant bodily experience?

Practice the following exercises so that you can begin to cultivate a flexible, mindful presence that will be increasingly available to you in the tough times.

Skill Practice: Ice Cubing Conflict

This activity will help you get a sense of what presence amid difficulties is all about.

With an ice cube, sit in a quiet place where you won't be disturbed. Hold the ice cube in an open palm and simply observe it.

Feel any and all sensations in your hand. Stinging, burning, pulsing—whatever sensations show up, just witness them without moving or doing anything.

Notice what your mind tells you. Maybe, "This is stupid," or, "Just toss it away," or something else. What does your mind suggest will happen if you continue to hold the ice cube? What does your mind want you to do with the ice as it becomes painful to hold it? Can you simply notice what your mind is saying and allow it to pass through your awareness, while continuing to hold the ice cube anyway?

What do you notice happening over the span of a minute or two? What's happening to the ice? Are things changing?

What does this suggest about what you can choose to do during painful experiences with your teen?

This activity is both metaphor and method. As a method, pausing in the midst of frustration to hold an ice cube can help you ride out your own emotional intensity without adding fuel to a bad situation. It's also a metaphor that reminds you that difficult, painful emotions *will* change if you let them. Yes, you'll end up with things to clean up (a wet hand, or a difficult situation unresolved), but that's far better than throwing the ice cube around and making things worse. It's not that you shouldn't take action when there's a problem to solve. But sometimes there's no problem—sometimes things just feel hard. Are you willing to "ice cube" your reactions and watch as things shift and change on their own?

The next time tough feelings about your teen's situation show up, try pausing in mindfulness to see another way forward. Let the ice cube practice remind you to hang in there with mindful presence even when the pain of parenting rises up in you.

More Than Deep: Anchoring with the Breath

Central to the PURE communication step of presence is to use your breathing to bring you fully into your bodily experience. Our breath is always here with us, but we tend to lose track of it when we become highly stressed, leading to high-chested, quick breaths that in turn increase the body's stress response. Such mindless reactive breathing pulls us out of presence.

With the following two exercises, we practice breathing deeply to anchor and stabilize you and help you connect with your teen.

Skill Practice: Redwood Respiration

Hyperion, the tallest tree in the world, is 397.7 feet tall. Hyperion is a redwood, an ancient species of tree that can live to be 2,000 years old. Contrary to what you might guess, a redwood's roots don't extend more than five or six feet into the earth. Instead, redwoods achieve their incredible stability by spreading roots out, up to a hundred feet away from the trunk.

This basic breathing practice, anchored in the metaphor of these majestic trees, will help you create stability amid teenage storms.

1. Take a slow, full breath in; breathe deep into your abdomen.

2. Imagine the breath continuing all the way down to your feet.

3. Exhale fully and then inhale again with another slow, penetrating breath.

4. Imagine the breath descending all the way to your feet; feel the sensations of your feet against the floor.

5. Exhale, inhale.

6. This time imagine the air pushing down from your feet and into the earth, then spreading far out in every direction. You are solid and stable, like an ancient redwood. The stability and calm you're creating with your breathing can stretch out to help stabilize others as well.

7. Continue to breathe deeply as you visualize this; know that even if the world around you surges with emotional intensity you can—and have—held up through many such storms.

Skill Practice: Math Breathing

For some people, the redwood respiration exercise may focus too much on imagination. Here's another breathing practice that doesn't require creative visualization, but will similarly help anchor you in mindful sensations of breathing. This technique is especially useful for counteracting a revved-up or upset state, and can be very helpful in times of stress with teens.

1. Pause wherever you are, standing or sitting, and notice where in your body you are breathing; for example, if you're upset or stressed, your breathing is likely to be primarily located in your chest.

2. For three seconds, inhale slowly and intentionally into your belly; fill your abdomen with breath.

3. Hold the breath in your belly for another count of three seconds. Gently notice the sensations in your body.

4. Slowly exhale for a count of six seconds, until the breath is completely expelled from your body.

5. Continue with this breathing math for several more cycles: 3+3=6. Three seconds inhaling. Three seconds holding. Six seconds exhaling. Be sure to breathe into the belly.

6. Notice the changes in your body after breathing this way. How does your state of mind now compare to your state of mind just before you started the exercise?

Ask Abblett

Q: I've heard people say "just take a deep breath" when things are stressful my whole life. But how is that actually going to help my kid not lash out and humiliate me in front of everyone at Thanksgiving dinner?

A: These breathing practices are meant to draw your attention away from raging thoughts and emotions and into the steady predictability of your breathing. Mindfulness of the breath can give you an anchor amid a storm, and conscious breathing can also have a significant soothing effect, allowing you to be that much more effective in your next move in a challenging situation.

Having an In-the-Body Experience During Tough Exchanges with Teens

If the Dalai Lama traded places with you and experienced an intense outburst from your teen, his body would register all that intensity with alarms not so different from yours. When asked in a *Time* interview if he experiences anger, His Holiness said, "Oh, yes, of course. I'm a human being. Generally speaking, if a human being never shows anger, then I think something's wrong. He's not right in the brain." He ended the statement with a chuckle (Gyatso 2010).

Forget the notion that anyone is born with perfect, nonreactive patience. Reactions happen. If we're not skilled in cultivating presence, they can scuttle our ability to respond in helpful ways to the agitation of our teen.

Throughout the book, as you work to connect with your teen, you will continue to turn your awareness to what's happening in your body. The next two exercises will help you become more present in your physical sensations. The more you learn to do so, the better you will be able to handle difficult interactions without what's happening in your body taking over.

Skill Practice: The SLOW Body Scan

With practice, you can do this body scanning exercise in a matter of seconds to slow yourself down and relax. This skill seems like commonsense, but it can elude your awareness during challenging moments with your teen. However, with practice, this skill can be rapidly executed, allowing you to claim its soothing benefits.

At each of the following four steps, pause for a moment with your awareness to feel that body part fully; consciously let go of any tension before moving on.

Stop: Stop what you are doing and soften the muscles of your face.

Lower: Lower your shoulders and your gaze.

Open: With your breath, open your chest and belly.

Wilt: Allow your whole body to wilt a little bit, to relax.

Repeat as necessary.

The SLOW body scan can be used daily to check in with your body and release any tension. Whether it's the knot in your stomach after your teen slams the front door, or your white-knuckled grip on the steering wheel after being cut off in traffic, you can SLOW and loosen your physical tension. Let your teen see you do it—show your teen how *you* handle emotional heat. Your teen will learn from your example.

Skill Practice: Fist Full o' Mindfulness

Adapted from "Open Hand Meditation" (Abblett 2013, 285)

We all grip our thoughts and emotions too tightly from time to time, particularly in stressful situations. School and work can be hard. Kids can pester you. A partner can be a pain. Whatever the reason, we all sometimes grip ourselves so tightly that emotionally we shut down and close up. This activity helps you observe tensions, slowly opening to experience until the tensions change on their own.

1. Sit in an upright, open posture.

2. Lay your hands gently on your thighs, palms up.

3. Take a few deep breaths. Feel your presence and calm in the place you're sitting.

4. When you're ready, close your eyes and focus your attention on the sensations of either your left or right hand.

5. Ball your hand into a fist and hold it as tightly as you can for several seconds. Release your hand. Repeat this process. And again.

6. Notice the difference between the feelings of tension and release.

7. Now, allow your hand to lie open in your lap. Notice the sensations showing up.

8. Don't just think about your hand. Instead, really sense the pulsing, the tingling, itching—whatever is present in the moment. Continue to notice what you're sensing, whether that's a sensation in the hand or another part of your body, or even a passing thought.

9. Notice how all of these experiences come, go, and change on their own.

10. Recognize that your hand can hold whatever sensations show up. So can you. With presence, when the stress of a moment shows up, you can simply hold it gently. It will come and go on its own.

As you repeat this exercise, try saying these phrases:

"Tension will show up as I deal with this—I can choose to let it go."

"Tough feelings may be there—I can watch them play themselves out until they go away of their own accord."

"Stress and bad feelings will probably return—I can always open my palm to them again."

Practice open hand meditation both in moments of calm and tension. Try to remember this activity during challenging interactions at home. No one need know as you silently tense and release your fist. Let the tension of the situation release just as the tensions in your hand does.

Seeing Clearly: Concentration and Clarity of Mind

When there's a lot happening at home, it's easy to become distracted and overwhelmed. When the mind is unfocused and emotions surge and swirl, we're more likely to say and do things that make situations develop in less than ideal ways. In the middle of chaos, it can be extremely useful to take a few seconds to center and steady awareness. A short balancing activity can help us find helpful resolutions for tough interactions.

Skill Practice: Unmoving Mind

This portable skill practice works on the same principle as does mastering the spinning teacup ride at an amusement park: find something in your line of sight that's perfectly still, and keep your focus there in order to avoid becoming dizzy and nauseated. When your teen is creating a tempest and you're noticing yourself getting mentally tossed about, this skill can help.

1. Scan your situation for something completely and perfectly still.

2. Allow your vision to rest on it.

3. In fact, let your mind settle *in* to it so that your mind becomes as still and unmoving as that object.

4. Acknowledge the choice you always have to direct your attention, and to choose stability and stillness, even when chaos and distraction abound.

5. Stay with the object for a few breaths, or even a few minutes if you have it.

6. Notice how effective your next action is relative to your typical action in such situations.

Skill Practice: Walking Away from Your Mind

What about when you just can't take it any more and discover you've already walked away from your teen? First of all, give yourself permission to take care of yourself. Instead of completely shutting down, allow yourself to go offline for a bit. You're not perfect and neither are your skills of presence. You can, however, turn this act of walking away itself into a mindfulness practice. Like the yogis of lore, you can walk the hot coals of the situation you're in.

After exiting a challenging or upsetting situation, as soon as you can, walk to a space where you aren't likely to be disturbed. Better yet, walk outside for a bit. This technique is much more than just taking a walk to cool off. This technique brings your mind back in touch with your body and back in touch with the firm ground around you.

1. Breathe in as you step forward with your right foot.

2. Exhale and slowly place your right foot on the ground; feel the sensations of your foot making contact with the ground.

3. Inhale and slowly step forward with your left foot.

4. Exhale and place your left foot down; again feel every sensation of the step forward.

5. Continue this slow, steady coordination of breath and movement; keep your mind laser-focused on what's happening in the soles of your feet.

6. Notice how, regardless of the speed of movement, you can elect to keep your mind grounded. You can experiment with increasing the pace or letting go of the coordination between breath and movement, but keep your mind concentrated on that feeling of contact with the earth.

Do this practice after moving away from your teen and you'll find yourself returning to your awareness faster and faster. Do this practice enough and you may find yourself no longer walking away at all.

Opening Up: Body Awareness Skills for Defeating Tunnel Vision

Many times in my work, I've observed talented staff members who, in working with challenging youth, become trapped by tunnel vision. Their perception of what's actually going on in a difficult situation narrows, often around a sense of blame, such as "Johnny is manipulating me," or, "Sarah is doing this on purpose!"

Tunnel vision can lead us to focus on just one causal conclusion, one explanation for what's making things happen. As a result, we can miss a whole host of other relevant factors. This is analogous to the limits of human vision. The electromagnetic spectrum includes a vast array of types of radiation, not just visible light. Our eyes, however, see only a tiny fraction of what's actually around us. It's easy to jump to the conclusion that what we see is all there is.

Parents of angry teens need to build a habit of asking, "What else?"—a habit of seeking a larger perspective in order to reduce rigid and reactive thinking. Teens can spot tunnel vision in adults, particularly their parents. Opening up to a wider angle lens, even for things that have little to do with your home life, is a valuable skill in and of itself. In chapter 3, we'll explore how to broaden perspective using mindfulness and positive psychology. Here, you'll begin to practice perspective by widening your awareness of your senses.

Skill Practice: Breathing Yourself Inside Out

When you're upset or overwhelmed, it can be hard to even notice what's happening, both in your body and in the world around you. Some people become distracted by the difficult circumstances happening around them. Others become focused on a particular unpleasant sensation in their body. All of that tensing, clenching, and distraction takes a toll on both your body and your brain—making it more likely you'll manage tough interactions with family in a less than ideal way.

Try this activity to connect to what's happening both inside and out.

1. Sit upright, comfortably—not tense or rigid.

2. Take three slow, deep breaths; let your mind focus on what it feels like to inhale. Where in your body do you feel it as you breathe in?

3. Notice and count at least five different sensations in different areas of your body. Don't focus on just one area. If you're tense in one place, try to notice sensations in other areas as well.

4. Continue to breathe slowly. Now, notice whether anything is changing in your body. Are the sensations you've noticed staying exactly the same, or are they shifting on their own?

5. Take three more slow, deep breaths. This time, let your mind focus on what it feels like to exhale. Where in your body do you feel it as you breathe out?

6. Notice and count at least five different things that you can see, hear, or touch where you are. Don't focus on just one thing; try to notice things all around you.

7. Continue to breathe slowly. How do you feel after going inside out?

Skill Practice: Fresh Eyes

This skill practice helps you break free of ingrained ways of viewing triggers—including your teen's actions and speech—as well as their stuff, which can clutter the home and become a nexus of conflict. The idea here is to see something fresh in the familiar.

1. Go into a space your teen frequently hangs out in. (Tread carefully if that's the teen's bedroom!) Pick an object your teen uses daily, particularly one you'd prefer the teen did not possess.

2. Explore this object with your complete attention. See and touch it. Inspect it with curiosity until you move past your

mental chatter of judgments and assumptions and notice something new about the object.

3. Later, apply the same observational curiosity to your teen. Don't poke or sniff your teen, but observe your teen until you notice something you have previously missed. Don't go looking for something negative. Instead, try to notice a detail about how your teen moves, speaks, or dresses that communicates something new.

4. Ask yourself: *What if I looked with eyes this fresh on a regular basis? What if my actions toward my teen were informed by this curiosity, these new impressions? What might be different in our interactions?*

The Parental Lap: Acceptance Skills for Holding the Good, the Bad, and the Otherwise

Decades ago, psychologist Martin Seligman and colleagues (Klein, Fencil-Morse, and Seligman 1976) documented the phenomenon of *learned helplessness*. Learned helplessness is a feeling of complete and absolute resignation in the face of negative inputs that do not seem to stop no matter what you do. Does this sound familiar? It has for many of the parents I've worked with. When faced with an onslaught of anger from a teen, for weeks, months, or even years, it is completely understandable to sink into a feeling of hopelessness or defeat.

When pain is here and now, it's important to rest into it rather than trying to fight it off. Do what you can to address and change a tough situation. Beyond that, acceptance—not resignation—can help you ride out the pain.

Acceptance is basically another way to look at presence itself. (Practicing acceptance is thus also a way to practice the other skills we've discussed in this chapter.) Acceptance is the full, nonjudgmental choice to rest in your moment-to-moment sense experience. The classic metaphor for understanding acceptance is that of quicksand. If you fall into a pit of quicksand, you have to consciously not do what your body and mind reflexively want to do—that is, flail about in panic. Instead, you have to lie back and rest into the quicksand, maximizing your surface area and floating. Doing so opens possible solutions for actually getting out of the trap you're in. If you're flailing about, you're much more likely to miss that stranger in the distance who could come over and yank you out. That's acceptance.

This chapter's final PURE presence practice offers you a strategy for building acceptance when the pain of a situation is not immediately going to change: take a NAPP.

Skill Practice: Taking a NAPP During Difficult Interactions

When you're in the midst of tough emotions like sadness, frustration, anger, hopelessness, and loneliness, struggling often only makes it worse. It's only when you relax into a painful moment that you have a chance to get unstuck.

NAPP is a method to help you float on the quicksand and create options for getting unstuck. It's a mantra you can repeat in the moment as well as a series of steps to both help you think more clearly about the situation you're in and keep from adding to your pain.

1.   Pause and **N**otice what's showing up in all your senses in the present moment. What are you hearing, seeing, touching, tasting, smelling, and thinking right now, regardless of how unpleasant it might be?

2.   **A**llow these sensations to be just as they are. Make the choice not to fight these sensations. Let yourself rest in the energy of the sensations in your body.

3.   Let these sensations and feelings fully **P**enetrate your awareness. Don't grab at them inside your mind—let them move on their own.

4. Stay put. Continue to notice and allow the sensations until they **P**ass away on their own. If they hang around, notice whether they have changed at all.

5. Repeat to yourself as needed: notice, allow, penetrate, pass. NAPP.

The idea here isn't for you to just suck it up and passively resign yourself to a bad situation. When you take a NAPP you choose to let go of struggling, to notice your bodily sensations rather than the hamster wheel of your mind. When you take a NAPP you ride things out until ideas for improving your situation become clear.

Fight to solve problems, but don't fight against your thoughts and feelings—it just doesn't work. Don't worry, you will still take action. However, you must cultivate mindfulness to manage situations effectively. Presence is the first step to improving communication with your teen.

The PURE method requires that you carry presence into each of the other steps. Like a board game sending you back to the start square, if something happens to dislodge your mindfulness, you must go back and start again. Go back to presence. This is why practice is so important. Mindfulness is central to moving beyond the heat with your teen.

Ask Abblett

Q: So with acceptance, I should just throw up my hands and get used to the fact that my child is a lost cause? That our family is broken?

A: Acceptance is about acknowledging the truth of what's already here. It doesn't say anything about what might be. Your flexibility, your ability to avoid reacting on autopilot, create the possibility of change. Resignation leaves no room for change.

Time Issues: Forget the Cushion, Just Practice!

All contemporary parents trip over time. It is impossible to fit everything in and get everything done in the daily twenty-four-hour pit-
tance we're allotted. You don't need a psychologist to tell you that.
However, sometimes we all need to be reminded to let go of our expectation that we should be getting everything done on time.

Again, the parental mind typically focuses on the future or past
and has difficulty with the present moment. Instead of worrying that
there will never be enough time to take on the skill practices of this
book, remember what is at stake here for your teen and for you. Can
you afford *not* to take the time to practice? Formal meditation on a
cushion every morning for forty-five minutes is not the point. Mindful
parenting doesn't mean trying to practice something you don't have
time for; it means minding the moments you're in. That is what the
majority of the practices in this book are about—being more fully
present in the moments of your parenting, however chaotic, intense, or
painful they may be.

That said, if you can carve out the time, a consistent meditation
practice can be helpful. Here are the basics of meditation. These basics
have stood the test of centuries and served millions of practitioners.

Peaceful Parent Practice: Meditation—
Taking Your "One Seat"

Psychologist, meditation teacher, and former Buddhist monk Jack
Kornfield (1993) has said that, with meditation, it's important to learn
to take your "one seat." That is, to find a method or practice and use it
consistently. There's a nearly endless array of meditation and mindfulness practices to choose from. It's easy to get lost in constant experi-
menting with new techniques (believe me, I've been there). What
follows is one of the most time-honored and simple seats for you to sit
your attention on.

Again, the goal of these Peaceful Parent Practices is to build yourself a firm foundation of mindfulness and positive self-management. This will allow you to rise to moments of difficulty and manage interactions with your teen with more flexibility, poise, and presence.

Follow these basic instructions for mindfulness meditation of the breath:

1. Find a quiet location where you won't be disturbed. Set a timer for three minutes.

2. Find a comfortable, alert posture, with your head and back upright and shoulders relaxed. Sit on a cushion or in a chair. Gently close your eyes.

3. Breathe naturally; don't worry about breathing slowly or deeply. Just breathe. Place your attention on the sensation of the breath.

4. Notice where you feel the breath most easily. Rest your attention on that particular sensation. For some people that's the nostrils. For others it's the throat or abdomen. Pick whatever feels most prominent for you.

5. Some beginners benefit from silently saying to themselves "in" when inhaling and "out" while exhaling. If this doesn't distract you from focusing on the sensation of the breath, doing so can help stabilize your attention.

6. You'll notice your mind trailing into thoughts, judgments, stories, aspects of past or future. Don't judge, label, or react negatively. Gently guide your attention back to the sensation of your breathing. The moment you catch yourself having wandered away into a thought is the moment you are mindful and present once more. This moment is crucial for building your skills of presence. Don't worry about how often this happens. Actually, the more the better—it means you're really building your muscle of mindfulness.

7. When the timer sounds, open your eyes. Give yourself credit for having experienced a valuable, ancient practice. Research has repeatedly shown that such meditation benefits our well-being, health, and effectiveness. Know that, even by practicing only for a few minutes, you've started down an important path of practice.

I recommend establishing a daily habit. Practice a sitting meditation such as this for at least three to five minutes to start. It usually helps to pick a consistent time and place. After several days, increase your sitting time to ten minutes. Try to work your way up to thirty consecutive minutes of meditation if possible. Again, don't use lack of time as an excuse for not doing the practices in this chapter. Do this sitting practice when and if you can. Over time, you'll notice benefits in terms of reduced tension as well as increased alertness, flexibility in thinking, and overall well-being.

Your Parental Agenda

Before you move on to the next chapter:

☐ If you haven't already, complete the parenting self-assessment. Note in your journal the mindfulness skill domains (such as anchoring and focus) that are most needed in your situation. Try to identify specific situations and behaviors from your teen that make a particular domain more challenging.

☐ Consult appendix A (available for download at http://www .newharbinger.com/35760) for further guidance in tailoring your presence practices to fit your needs.

☐ Take your "one seat" with a daily meditation practice.

3 Understanding: Creating Clarity in the Cycle of Teen Anger

You can practice mindfulness meditation in a cave in the Himalayas for decades, but if you don't develop your capacity to understand your teen's suffering, your ability to change your reactions in the face of your teen's anger will be limited. This chapter stands firmly on the foundation of mindful presence to teach you to look "behind" your teen's angry behavior with the compassion your relationship requires.

In this chapter you will:

- Build your willingness and skill to draw on the values that fuel you as a parent, even in the face of significant difficulty.

- Engage in practices designed to create flexibility in your perspective regarding your teen *and* yourself.

- Enhance your willingness and skill to emotionally tune into your teen, particularly when your relationship feels far from close or collaborative.

The Core Question: Are You Willing?

Near a monastery in the forests of Thailand grows a tree bearing a plaque. The plaque reads: "If you have something bad smelling in your pocket, wherever you go it will smell bad. Don't blame it on the place." The monastery's abbot, Ajahn Chah, may not have been thinking of modern Western parents when he said this, but the wisdom applies just the same.

When faced with an angry or out-of-control teenager, it's very easy to blame the "smell" of things on the badness coming from the teen. But we, as parents, bring our bad smells with us as well. This chapter focuses on learning to see both what's good and what's not so good in our own internal inventories as parents, as well as what's happening behind an angry teen's behavior. Clearly seeing patterns that help and hinder communication is crucial to helping your child.

I'm reminded of a baseball game and a parent and teen I worked with some years ago. It's an example where teen anger and parental patterns—and therapist's patterns, too—were all heavily involved.

From the bleachers I watched my school's angry heavy hitter come to the plate. "Swing away, Russ," his coach called. In the time I'd known Russell, I'd never heard anyone, not even his mom, call him "Russ." In a few months that coach had gotten closer than I had in three years of intensive work.

As I took in the family onlookers around me, I found myself thinking that none of these people—including his coach—had any concept of Russell's true behavior. They didn't know Russell's angry outbursts, they didn't know how Russell would get in others' faces, swearing with fists raised. They only saw a kid doing his best to assume the proper stance, trying to connect with the ball. I knew the truth.

There was no sign of Russell's mom. By the fourth inning it was safe to say she wasn't coming. She'd had enough of Russell's tantrums at home, the threats and holes in her walls. Russell's unsafe behavior and his mom's inability to monitor him had led me to recommend Russell be placed in a residential therapeutic program.

While it was true that Russell's neighborhood BB gun wars and angry battles with his mom were toxic and potentially dangerous, it was also true that my motivations for recommending the residential program were mixed. As T.S. Eliot writes, the "last temptation is the greatest treason: to do the right deed for the wrong reason." I hadn't been able to stand the anxiety and helplessness Russell's intensity triggered in me.

Here was a teen looking to pin adults' attention to him with the force of his fury. And here were the teen's mother and therapist, each acting out familiar scripts of ducking and covering, of avoiding Russell's intensity.

Working with Russell—and others in my caseload—almost led me to quit and slink away, away from the difficult situations, away from the anger pointed daggerlike in my direction. Thankfully, I've improved my ability to stay with my emotional discomfort when working with clients' challenging behavior. I've grown, thanks to considerable practice of skills such as those in this book, as well as to support from others. My old pattern of avoiding others' anger still tugs at me, but I no longer reactively follow it as often. Emotional patterns don't go away, not for any of us. Rather, we must turn and face them with awareness.

I used to have a picture of a high-jump skier tacked to the wall of my office. Even before Sheryl Sandberg had made the phrase famous in her book of the same name, I captioned the picture on my wall, "Lean in." When clients or colleagues in my office were facing an emotional challenge and their patterns tugged at them to turn away or push back reactively, I suggested they lean in. In order to lean into something difficult—such as taking a brutally honest look at your own internal stories and patterns that may be getting in the way of improving your relationship with your teen—it's crucial to ask yourself a simple question: *am I willing?*

Identifying Your True North as a Parent

As you work through this book, as you do your best to help your teenager resolve anger-related problems, you will often feel lost and unsure of yourself. Part of the second step of the PURE method—understanding—comes from creating clarity as to what drives you as a parent. Becoming clear on what matters most for you will deepen your role as a relational leader for your teen. The core values behind your decisions as a parent—including your missteps—can help pull you forward and answer yes to the willingness question. After you've worked to identify these values and make them accessible, in challenging moments they can become a sort of magnetic north, offering you guidance.

To help you identify the values that give your parenting direction, let's take a quick detour from parenting and go back to school.

Skill Practice: Your Greatest Teacher

1. Sit in a quiet place and close your eyes. Take a breath and remember how your breathing has always been there inside and around you. Your breath is your constant companion, there to help your body adjust to whatever the situation requires.

2. When you were a kid in school, there was a teacher who really mattered to you. A teacher you most admired. A teacher who had the greatest positive impact on you. Let your mind gravitate toward this teacher. Imagine this person clearly, using multiple senses. Remember exactly what the teacher did or said that hit the mark for you.

3. What, specifically, were this teacher's actions toward you? What qualities kept showing up in the teacher's teaching and interactions? Don't just think about it—allow yourself to really feel your answers as they show up.

4. Open your eyes. Note these specific actions and qualities in your journal. Write down as many things as possible that made this teacher special for you.

5. Pause for a moment and notice how you feel. What's showing up for you as you remember this teacher? To what degree did you want to perform well for this person? To what degree did you want to be in this person's presence? How much did you end up learning?

6. Notice the qualities you listed in step 4. How important are these for *you* to embody in your role as a parent? If they're

important to you *and* you embody them, what might be the impact on your teen?

7. Consider embracing your teacher's qualities as guiding values for you as a parent. You are not your teen's formal educator, but you are the teacher your teen will learn from the most.

We're working here to identify and create more ready avenues for you to access these values. No one and no book can create these values for you—they are already there. If you are willing to understand what they have to show you, these values are ready to guide you. Authenticity, compassion, perseverance, generosity—whatever they are, you need only be willing to let yourself move toward them when opportunities arise.

A Chinese proverb tells us, "Pearls don't lie on the seashore. If you want one, you must dive for it." Living our values entails taking a risk. We risk the pain of falling short in our parenting. But if we don't take that risk, we'll have nothing of true value to pass along to our children. Let's turn now to another values-clarification exercise, this time focusing specifically on your teen.

Skill Practice: Your Teen's Commencement Speech

1. Close your eyes and imagine that you're sitting in a huge auditorium. It's graduation day for your teen. Hundreds of people sit in bleachers all around you.

2. This ceremony has a unique importance for you: your teen is delivering one of the commencement speeches. Your teen approaches the lectern and looks straight at you.

3. Your teen speaks from the heart about your actions and who you are as a person—the things that have mattered that helped

your teen get to this important day. Visualize this scene in as much detail as possible. Ask yourself, *What do you want your child to say? What do you, in your deepest heart, want to hear your teen say about what you did that mattered—and perhaps to you too?*

4. Whatever actions or qualities you've imagined your teen talking about—and no one can tell you what they are; again, they are part of who you are—list them in a journal or on a piece of paper. Focus on actions or qualities you can do in an ongoing way, such as "being engaged," or, "giving support," or, "championing my teen's dreams." Focus less on individual outcomes, such as "taught my teen to drive a car," or, "got my teen into a good college." It's the ongoing things you most want to hear about, right? The things you were doing regularly that really mattered. These actions and qualities serve as directions that are always there to guide you as a parent.

Note that these are not goals, not things you check off your to-do list so you can move on. They're things you keep showing up to do and that you do simply because they matter. These are true directions, like headings on a compass. You're never really done with these; rather, you just keep moving in these directions. Are you willing to let your values emerge as clearly as your teen's voice at commencement?

Skill Practice: Forget Silver Linings— Go for Gold with Your Teen

Positive psychology research consistently shows that cultivating feelings of gratitude leads to positive outcomes in well-being and happiness. Here, we will begin a practice you can return to regularly to cultivate this attitude with regard to your relationship with your teen. This practice also serves to help you continue to clarify the values underlying your parenting.

1. Consider a specific way or situation in which things are blocked or broken down with your teen. Think about what seems to always get missed or misunderstood. Look at the moment when things seem to go awry.

2. People have probably suggested you find the silver lining when things are hard. "Oh, at least you have your health," or, "But look at how smart your kid is—Harvard-bound for sure," or, "No one can have it all, just think about everything else in your life that's working so well." Forget all that. Discard all these warm and fuzzy distractions. Instead, lean your attention directly into the communication breakdown with your teen.

3. Ask yourself: *How is this situation with my teen a gift to the parent inside I most want to embody?* Core feelings and needs drive things to get stuck between you and your teen. This stuckness is a gift, a wake-up call to help you establish a meaningful and lasting connection.

4. Are you willing to view this situation as a gift? A growth mindset asks you to consider that change is possible and will come—even if you can't see how or when just yet—particularly if you're willing to approach breakdowns with an attitude of gratitude. Try it: hold this breakdown in a moment of felt gratitude. Might your teen notice this shift in your perspective? What impact might this have?

No skier goes over the lip of a ramp (Olympic ramps are 394 feet in elevation!) without at least a moment of willingness. No one shoves a skier over the edge. And no one can make you look deeply into your own emotional patterns. That's why this chapter asks you to pause and really consider the question: *Are you willing?* Are you? It's fine if you say no, just know that this may carry some costs. It's to these costs we will turn next.

Ask Abblett

Q: How does identifying my parental values help when my kid is out of control?

A: Identifying your values is not an intellectual exercise that gives you insights or solutions. Knowing your values, however, gives you an emotional nudge toward what matters most, even in the heat of the moment with your kid. Your values show you your highest self as a parent. Being able to identify and focus on them can help steady you as you progress through the methods of this book.

The Costs of Miscommunication

In chapter 1 we discussed how our brain's anatomy makes anger and reactivity universal, even though these often get in our way. But there's more to the story than just the firing of neurons in the brains of parents and kids. Part of what leads everyone involved to feel hopeless and stuck is a pattern of communication that tends to build up over time.

As we also discussed in chapter 1, coercive cycles can build up between parents and kids through a process of mutual reinforcement and punishment. These coercive cycles are unplanned, and yet very destructive communication breakdowns between teens and parents. It's the *relationship* here—not the teen, nor any power moves, oppositionality, or manipulation—that is the problem. Either the parent, the teen, or both can initiate the cycle, leading to increased anger and solidifying the negative pattern.

Consider this anonymous quote: "Your thoughts become your words. Words become your behavior. Behavior becomes your habits. Habits become your values. Values become your destiny." Momentum can grow from the smallest of internal experiences. Untended, our thoughts can evolve into either the brightest or darkest aspects of our character. Over time, our thoughts coalesce into the emotional inheritances we pass on to our children.

Recently I worked with a mother of a teenaged girl who had significant learning, emotional, and behavioral challenges. The mom herself had struggled with mood-related difficulties throughout her life. Over the years, this mother and daughter had become increasingly entrenched in a destructive dance, with escalations taking the whole family hostage and threatening the well-being of siblings and the woman's spouse.

"After that last explosion from her," the mother said, "something snapped in me, or maybe more like died. Now, when she starts yelling, badgering her sister or bringing up awful things I've done in the past, I don't lash out in anger like I used to."

I told her this was good—being able to contain the anger and resentment her daughter's behavior caused was a step in the right direction.

"The problem is," she continued, "I don't feel anything for her anymore. I just don't care. So I just sit there and don't react no matter what she does."

What at first had sounded like an adaptive, healthy change was actually a serious turn for the worse. Yes, this mom no longer flared at her daughter, but at a cost—it was if she had died as a parent. And now this girl had to come home from school and watch her mom go on living with everyone but her.

"She can't keep doing this to me," the mother told me. "She keeps me on the hook for the mistakes I've made. But you can only allow yourself to be abused so many times before it's time to leave. Divorces have to happen sometimes. Brutal bosses should expect victimized employees to quit."

"You have to ask yourself," I told her, "what will be the cost if things stay dead like they are? What will you lose that will matter a great deal? And are you okay with that?"

I was asking this mom to step aside from the resentment and self-protection that, understandably, had a stranglehold on her parental heart. I asked, "Are you able to just watch what your mind is doing right now?"

The goal of the exercise was for her to wander her way to something that resonated with her—something more important than her attempts to control and force away her pain.

I asked this mom to imagine her daughter was sitting in the empty chair across from her. "It's the last chance you have to talk to her. She doesn't know it, but you know you will die tomorrow. The how doesn't matter, but you know it, with certainty." I looked at her, pausing to allow this to settle in.

"It's the last full breath of your life. What will you say?"

All parents—this mother and myself included—build up expectations, assumptions, and judgments based on what our kids and the contexts we live in bring us. Our feelings of being overwhelmed can blind us to possible pathways forward with our teens. Rigid thoughts inside can feel more real than the teen actually standing in front of us, face pained and desperately hoping.

Truth was, this mother was waiting to feel differently before she would change her actions. She was doing what many of us do, particularly when we've been sufficiently burned in our relationships. We let a numbness of heart block us from doing anything to break the patterns that have generated so much momentum, thinking things like, *I can't reach out to them because I don't feel like it.*

Emotions often *follow* behavior. When we do things, feelings tend to trail along in their wake. Minds, because they are slow on the uptake, fool us into thinking the causal chain goes in the other direction. Depressed people wait for their mood to shift before they attempt to engage in life once again. Anxious folks wait for calm before they step out into the unknown. And overwhelmed, burned-out parents wait to feel connection again, to feel at least a flicker of compassion and caring before they reach out toward their "oppositional" teen.

What if the teens are waiting as well? Waiting for us to lead them away from this reactivity we're silently yet powerfully passing on to them? They are our children, they have no choice but to be the heirs of our actions. Potentially, as parents themselves, they will have to consider what inheritance will go to their own children, and so on.

What if we, the deadened parents, were willing to ignore our numbed or resentful minds and move ourselves in the direction of our children? Would they notice the change, the shift in our patterns? What message might that send?

Remember, you did not choose your brain's anatomical structure; the subtle, mutual shaping of a coercive cycle with your teen; or the genetic and learned inheritance of emotional patterns from your own parents. You did not choose the patterns in which you and your teen are ensnared. But you can learn to manage them responsibly. You can practice PURE communication methods for sidestepping old reactivity and finding new patterns, leading toward less anger and more connection with your teen.

Skill Practice: More Than Our Stories as Parents

1. With something to write on, set a timer for one minute. In that time, as rapidly as possible, list as many positive attributes or qualities about yourself as a parent that you can.

2. Set your timer for another minute. Do the same for your negative qualities as a parent. Again, write them down as quickly as you can.

3. Close your eyes and take a few centering breaths; perhaps practice the 3+3=6 Math Breathing exercise from chapter 2.

4. Open your eyes. Survey both lists. These lists basically summarize the story you tell yourself about your role as a parent. Notice how it feels to read your story.

5. Ask yourself: *Is this story sufficient? Does it fully describe who I am as a parent in every possible situation? Are there things left unaccounted for here?*

This chapter teaches a deeper understanding of the inner narrative driving communication between you and your teen. Particularly in the tougher moments, you've likely been buying in to your inner story as if it's absolute truth. You believe it with holy book intensity. We all fall into this tendency at various points. Check in with yourself about how things tend to go when you cling to your story too tightly, whether what you're clinging to is the good stuff or the not-so-good stuff. Are you willing to loosen your mental and emotional grip on this narrative about yourself? What happens in your parenting when you do?

The Heirs of Our Actions: Emotional Patterns in Parenting

Psychologists (Gottman, Katz, and Hooven 1996) have introduced the concept of *parental meta-emotional philosophy*. Your parental meta-emotional philosophy is the accumulated set of feelings and thoughts you have about both your own emotions and the emotions of your children. Again, parents are their children's greatest models of emotional and social competence. Parents play a major role in the emotional socialization of their children, helping them to label, understand, and manage emotions (Stettler and Katz 2014). Through both direct observation and modeling, parents' emotional behaviors and expressiveness influence their children (Halberstadt, Crisp, and Eaton 1999). While children also learn indirectly from various emotion-eliciting social situations—for example, at school, in the neighborhood, during extracurricular activities—parental influence is often viewed as the most significant (Hakim-Larson et al. 2006).

Gottman and colleagues (1996) propose that what parents think and feel about emotions in themselves and their children—their parental meta-emotional philosophy—is related to how they shape emotion in their kids. This research highlights four styles of meta-emotional philosophy. The *emotion coaching* style involves adaptive parenting. Parents are both aware of feelings and actively help their children process their feelings, offering appropriate labels and validation, as well as guidance for managing them. The *laissez-faire* style similarly includes awareness and acceptance of children's emotions; however, parents using this style are less likely to set limits or teach children how to resolve difficulties that arise. The *dismissing* style ignores and trivializes children's negative emotions. Consequently, children get the message that they should disregard their own emotional experiences, which can lead to difficulties in learning to regulate their feelings. The *disapproving* style involves a similar lack of acceptance, but parents with this style also actively criticize their children's displays of negative emotions, often punishing children for showing their feelings openly. This can create significant obstacles for these children with regard to accepting and managing their own emotional experiences, sometimes for years to come.

Science now links the patterns of managing and expressing emotion that children learn from their caregivers to later outcomes, sometimes extending much later into adulthood. Thus, for example, such patterns can affect future parenting practices (Gottman and Carrere 1999), increase self-soothing in children (Gottman, Katz, and Hooven 1996), yield more successful friendships and romantic relationships (Simpson et al. 2007), and contribute to the intergenerational transmission of abuse to subsequent generations (Duffy and Momirov 2000).

When it comes to understanding your emotional patterning, a great deal is at stake. There's what happens with your teen's anger in the immediate sense, and then there's the patterning the teen will carry into the future as your emotional heir, and likely as a parent as well.

Understanding Your Own Emotional Patterning

As a kid, I loved my mom's compassion—my mom was the closest thing in real life to June Cleaver from *Leave It to Beaver*—and it often helped me. But not on one particular day. That day I didn't want to get out of her car. I wanted to quit Little League.

"You dropped it, Abblett!" The face of Mr. Pencher, my coach, always had the look of an impending aneurysm when he spoke to me. "You gotta get under it. Don't be scared of it!" I hated him almost as much as I hated myself for how much I sucked at baseball. I just couldn't get on top of the jitters I felt as I stepped up to the plate or watched a fly ball hang like a massive moth up in the lights until it quickly flew down at me. It's not easy to see a ball with tears brimming.

In the car that day, I looked over at Mom and rammed my sweating palm deeper into my glove. "I want to go home," I said. My mom tried to nudge me to stay, "Don't you want to play with your friends?" But this only reminded me of how they would all shake their heads when I dropped yet another ball. Anxiety swelled. I turned on the tears. "No, don't make me stay." Before I knew it, I was homeward bound. Spider Man comics would be my faithful solace.

And so it went, across hundreds of situations: I would encounter something intimidating or upsetting and, if I pitched enough of a fit, my mom would smooth things over. I would get to sidestep the issue and move on. These interactions helped ingrain a pattern of avoidance in me.

Much later in my life, as clinical director of a therapeutic day school for children with emotional and behavioral issues, I would regularly witness kids in the midst of volcano-like tantrums or extreme states of agitation. I've seen kids swear, kick, spit, punch, break everything in sight. And I've seen those trying to care for these kids struggle with the emotional impact of their proximity to all this intensity. And then there was me: a guy from a household where anger and volatile emotion were to be avoided at all costs. Though it depended somewhat on the situation, anger and conflict were definitely taboo. I had developed a keen radar for conflict and had learned how to sidestep it before anger could spark.

You can imagine the challenges I experienced when I first began a job where conflict was a regular guest in my schedule. When I was paged because a child was in a significant behavioral crisis—screaming, crying, swearing, and yelling—my anxiety would surge and I would want nothing more than to walk—or run—in the other direction. This avoidance pattern was woefully unworkable.

We're not after insight into the origin of these patterns or scripts here. It doesn't matter much whether mommy or daddy did or didn't do such and such, or what this might say about your tendencies toward lollipops or messy desktops. My old pattern of avoidance is not my mom's fault. Indeed, such thinking is not only unhelpful, it helps maintain the pattern. Ask yourself, *If I learned my unhelpful pattern from my parents, where did they learn it?* Keep asking and you'll find there's no one person on the other end of the finger you're pointing.

So what do we do about these patterns that block us in our parenting? Making progress on these patterns comes down to our willingness to get a full sense of the here-and-now impact of the pattern. To get a full sense of our willingness to understand what is happening *now* inside ourselves during interactions with family, to understand how our minds are molding the thoughts and emotions we experience in the present moment.

Skill Practice: Your Style of Managing Negative Emotions

In quiet meditation, ask yourself the following questions. Don't sit analyzing your answers. Instead, gently and without judgment, notice what emerges in your thoughts and emotions as you slowly pose each question. You can pose just a single question for a given period of contemplation, or you can pose multiple questions and see how they influence one another. The point here is to cultivate a stance of compassionate *curiosity* as to the patterns that underlie your emotions, particularly the negative emotions sparked by the current situation with your teen.

When you are sad or lonely, how do you tend to treat yourself?

When fear builds inside you, what do you tell yourself about it? What do you feel you need to do?

When restlessness and anxiety brim, how do you respond?

When anger either swells inside you or is directed at you, what is your immediate inclination?

When you are confused and feeling overwhelmed, what does your mind lead you toward? What do you end up doing?

For any of the emotions above, in what direction are you pulled— toward them, away from them, or against them?

Are you able to open to these experiences, or do you tend to close in some way? How do you close? How, specifically, might you open?

Next, take a moment and write the following blank table in your journal:

	Open	Close
Sadness		
Fear		
Anger		
Anxiety		
Confusion		

Now, for each emotion, rate how willing you are to open to or move into painful sensations versus how much you tend to close down or move away from or against such sensations. It's not that you should never close to emotional experiences. Indeed, sometimes, such as in the middle of an immense crisis, it can be helpful to do so in order to address the situation. Here, though, we're interested in your general tendencies toward these emotions. The more closed your patterns are, the more work you'll want to do to create flexibility, so that you can help your teen do so as well.

Ask Abblett

Q: After spending some time with this material on emotional patterning, I'm feeling pretty hopeless. How can I possibly do anything to sidestep this wave of reactivity that's been carried across multiple generations in my family?

A: Instead of focusing on judging yourself and your family for these patterns, is there any room for compassion toward yourself? Toward your parents and grandparents? What would you say to a close friend struggling to come to terms with reactive patterns in their parenting?

Sticks and Stones: Understanding How Teen Behavior Affects the Parent

We've shed some light on patterns of emotionality that may be adding to the reactive mix for you and your teen. Now, let's explore a tool for increasing your in-the-moment understanding of what is happening between you two and what you might do—in the PURE sense—to address it.

I created the following Relational Compass primarily to train therapists. But, in addition to being an excellent way to assess exchanges between therapists and clients, it's also a great tool for assessing exchanges between parents and teens. The Relational Compass helps you take what you learned about your meta-emotional styles in the preceding contemplation exercises and put that into an interpersonal, here-and-now context. Do your habits of reaction to your teen—or anyone—lead you to connect or disconnect from the other person's perspective and needs? Are these habits things you do in an external or observable sense, or are they internal, such as thoughts and feelings?

The Relational Compass helps you sort your habits into patterns so that you can start to use mindful understanding to catch them as they arise. Once you recognize your patterns, you can then apply your various skills of presence and understanding to create choice and flexibility in your responses. This can both break coercive cycles and help interactions move in a better, less angry direction.

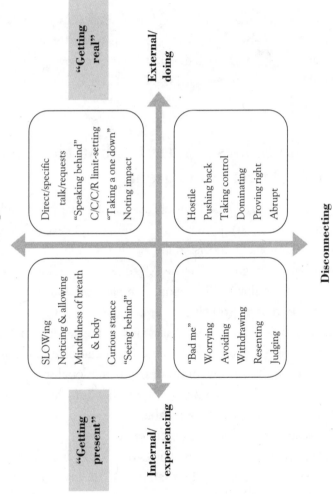

The Relational Compass©

Connecting

"Getting real"

External/ doing

Direct/specific
talk/requests
"Speaking behind"
C/C/C/R limit-setting
"Taking a one down"
Noting impact

Hostile
Pushing back
Taking control
Dominating
Proving right
Abrupt

Disconnecting

SLOWing
Noticing & allowing
Mindfulness of breath
& body
Curious stance
"Seeing behind"

"Bad me"
Worrying
Avoiding
Withdrawing
Resenting
Judging

"Getting present"

Internal/ experiencing

Figure 3.1: The Relational Compass

Spend some time studying the Relational Compass. The top two quadrants include PURE skills with the familiar presence and understanding skills in the top left and responsive leadership and empowerment skills—which we'll cover in the coming chapters—in the top right.

Now that you have a general sense of the Relational Compass, it's time to start using it.

Skill Practice: Noticing the Pull Toward Unhelpful Reactivity

The following practice is meant to be used both offline and online with your teen. The goal is to use the Relational Compass to identify the specific situational and behavioral triggers that spark your unhelpful reactive patterns, beginning a coercive cycle.

Offline practice:

1. Choose a recent conflict or anger-related situation with your teen.

2. In a quiet location, practice a few minutes of mindful breathing as we've practiced throughout the book.

3. With eyes closed, call to mind the episode with your teen. Imagine it in full sensory detail.

4. Notice what's happening around you—what's said, what's done, as well as things like time of day, who else is present, etc.

5. Notice what's happening in your thoughts and emotional reactions.

6. Notice any impulses you may have to close down.

7. Open your eyes. Using the Relational Compass as a categorizing tool, take a few minutes to review the episode, sorting both your reactions and your teen's.

8. Record what you have learned with regard to triggering factors and your own patterning in your journal.

Online practice:

1. In the midst of a mild-to-moderate episode with your teen (for safety reasons, don't practice this during the most severe episodes), notice any evidence in your body and thoughts that you are closing in a reactive, rigid, or rapid way. How are you flaring or fleeing—or experiencing the impulse to do so?

2. If possible, remove yourself from the situation and sit for a few minutes.

3. Work through steps 2 through 8 from the offline practice above.

4. Give yourself credit for demonstrating sufficient PURE skills to notice your reactions and interrupt the pattern long enough to work on understanding it more fully!

Continue this sort of data collection across days and weeks if possible.

The more you assume the perspective of a curious observer of your own patterning, the more the patterns will shift in a positive direction. Sometimes, just looking helps detangle and loosen things. The next practice will help you set the stage for more helpful responses to your teen's anger.

Skill Practice:
Pushing at Unhelpful Patterns

This practice is adapted from the work of meditation teacher Ken McLeod. In *Wake Up to Your Life* (2002), McLeod writes of the value of learning to mindfully hold one's reactive patterns—to use awareness to pause the mindless onslaught of our conditioning.

1. Do steps 1 through 5 of the preceding offline practice sequence in order to establish mindful awareness of a visualized, yet real, exchange with your teen.

2. Instead of just watching the cycle play out as usual, visualize yourself *pushing* on the pattern by doing something differently. Imagine yourself doing and saying something that opens you to the difficult aspects of the experience.

3. Use mindfulness to simply notice and allow whatever shows up. Observe what happens in mind and body without judgment or labeling.

4. Do not identify with the patterns. See the patterns as things that can change and shift like everything else. It's not you doing them. *They* are doing *you*.

5. Ask yourself: *Are the original, closing, reactive patterns serving my values as a parent?*

6. Ask yourself: *Are the imagined, new, open responses serving my values?*

7. Notice how you feel as you wrap up the exercise. Journal your observations.

In this chapter, we've identified how emotional patterning affects coercive cycles and miscommunication. We've practiced tools for recognizing and assessing these patterns as they show up in heated moments. Now, we will develop a key understanding skill: using mindfulness to shift how you relate to your own thinking—particularly thinking that keeps you on the treadmill of distress with your teen.

The Universal Errors in How We See Bad Behavior

When was the last time someone cut you off in traffic on purpose? When people do things that upset, displace, injure, or offend us, we often unthinkingly assume they intended to do it. I know I fall into this trap time and time again. Just a few weeks ago, a bus driver swerved into my lane, almost shoving me off the road. "He clearly saw me," I said to myself. "What a jerk!"

Social psychologists have documented that humans tend to make a perceptual error called *correspondence bias* (Gilbert and Malone 1995). The essence of correspondence bias is the observer's incorrect view of the actor's control over circumstances. Correspondence bias leads us to assume that others' behavior is a result of their internal traits and intentional choices—particularly with regard to negative behaviors like aggressive driving, substance abuse, or being irritable with coworkers. The human brain, in its role as observer, seems to take a mental shortcut. Instead of considering the many possible contextual factors that may have caused the behavior, be it another's gestures, tone of voice, the influence of peers and family, or even the weather, our brain jumps ahead and shoves the behavior into a category: "He's lazy, that's why he didn't turn in his homework." "She's an addict. Of course she destroyed her marriage." This shortcut saves time and frees our brain to update our Facebook page or watch *The Voice*. Imagine how bogged down your mind would be if you always considered every nuance, every possible factor of others' behavior. You'd end up snarled in your own mental traffic.

Ask yourself: *What is the difference between the needs of kids at a cancer center and kids with significant emotional problems who throw tantrums?* I believe the difference exists primarily in perception. Kids fighting cancer are, deservedly so, "empathy easy." The kids I work with as a psychologist—and perhaps your teen as well—the kids who swear, kick, punch, refuse, and fail, are "empathy hard." What's crucial to understand, however, is these "unruly" kids are no less deserving of empathy.

In the years I've spent working with such kids, I've found myself prone to making certain assumptions. After a particularly dramatic display—f-bombs, middle fingers, whatever—I've caught myself entertaining phrases such as "attention-seeking," "manipulative," "oppositional," or perhaps simply, "this kid is being a pain in the ass." Sometimes I question such responses and realize I've fallen prey, again, to this universal yet reversible limitation of human perception. Our perspective as observers of others' behavior can blind us. The same perceptual limitations get in the way of our parenting. The bad we see in our teen's behavior can sometimes harden the very center of our hearts.

When looking at others, unless clear external factors leave the person blameless (such as the young child with cancer who did nothing to create the situation), we tend to assume that a behavior is the inevitable result of a person's own internal traits. The person who cuts us off in traffic is a jerk. The colleague who walks out of the office in a huff has an attitude problem. They *chose* and therefore *caused* this behavior. It's easy to see how our compassion—and consequently the efficacy of our communication—can then falter.

Distancing Yourself from Distorted Thinking About Your Teen

When faced with a teen's anger, a torrent of thoughts run through the parental mind: *Here we go again. I can't believe she's losing it over something so ridiculous! Why does she always have to do this. I'm so sick of walking on eggshells. She's really manipulating the hell out of me. No way I'm letting her screw with me this time.* (Add your own examples, perhaps plus an expletive or two.)

While these thoughts are completely understandable, particularly in the midst of an angry interaction, the emotional charge here suggests a problematic rigidity. The thoughts present themselves as real and accurate. They show a totally reasonable sense of unfair treatment at the hands of your teen. And they often imply an absolute aspect of time with words like "never" and "always." While rigidity, truth assumptions, unfairness, and permanency may reflect the difficulty of the situation with your teen, how effective are you when you dwell on these qualities? Do thoughts infused with these characteristics help or hinder your ability to manage the moment?

An alternative is to build flexibility into how you relate to your own thoughts. Understanding requires a heaping helping of mindful awareness of thinking—of observing your own thoughts without either buying into them as absolute truth or trying to force them away. Try telling yourself *not* to think about how you've failed as a parent. Do it right now. Don't let yourself think about it, not even a little bit! Pointless, right? You can't force thoughts away, particularly ones with energy and momentum behind them.

What's more helpful is to build your capacity to serve as a witness to your own thoughts. Can you notice yourself thinking right now? Pause and try it. Can you observe your own inner voice? The moment you try to do so, you are in understanding: you are mindful of your thoughts, instead of being the thoughts. Typically, when parents think about how they have failed, that thought feels very close, as if it's inside them, part of who they are. Mindfulness helps you see the thought as merely a moment of information. It's just a thought. Just one of the thousands your mind churns out on a daily basis.

Key to understanding is learning to watch your own thinking, to notice that thoughts come and go on their own. This sounds simple, yet takes considerable practice. Like bubbles you've blown, thoughts are just there: they float around a bit and eventually drift away and pop or disappear.

Skill Practice: Going BMW
with Your Thoughts

Though I've never owned one, I've had occasion to drive a BMW sedan. It's an experience that sucks you in; you can lose yourself in the desire to possess such a car. In contrast to BMWs, I've owned many thoughts over the course of my life. That is, I've regarded thoughts about my foibles, failures, and frustrations as being part of me. However, I've learned that I feel better and am much more effective when I simply "drive" a thought instead. When I see a thought as a means of trying to make sense of things, rather than as part of who I am, I don't get sucked in. I relate to the thought, but the thought doesn't bind me.

I call this going BMW: going *Behind* the *Mind* and *Watching*. During, after, or even while anticipating an episode with your teen, try the following to get behind your thinking and become your own witness.

1. Recognize to yourself, *I'm having the thought that* _____ [insert rigid thought]. This will help you step back and watch the thought. This is very different than arguing with a thought or trying to force a thought away.

2. Think to yourself, *Thanks, mind, for coming up with* _____ [insert thought].

3. Take a breath and mentally place the thought in the corner of the room. Visualize the shape, color, size, movement, and sounds that describe the thought. For a few breaths, just watch it there in the corner.

4. Ever see Charlie Brown cartoons? Remember how the teacher sounded to the kids? *Wah, wah wah wah wah!* Take the highly charged thought your mind is zapping you with and imagine that, instead of "you" saying it, it's that cartoon teacher saying it instead. Give the thought the same amount of attention the *Peanuts* kids did to their poor teacher.

5. Think the thought *very slowly*, as if it's a recording on a scratched CD.

6. Regard the thought as if it's a car passing you, as you, the witness, merely drive alongside.

The goal with all of these techniques is to shift from a rigid, absolute frame of thinking to foster instead a more flexible relationship with your mental experience. This requires a lot of practice. To be of real benefit, this practice must become a habit. Such a habit will give you a measure of psychological freedom amidst even the most challenging provocations.

Learning to See Behind Behavior

The next set of practices builds off your mindful presence of your sense experiences, as well as the understanding you've acquired of your thoughts and emotional patterns. Once you can accomplish this, you open up the possibility of seeing behind your teen's behavior in a compassionate way. This is the heart of the PURE method. You're taking it all in. You're not reacting—or, at least, you're not reacting as much as you have in the past. You're able to bring in and authentically hold what's driving things for your teen. You're getting past the hard aspects of correspondence bias and seeing what deserves some empathy.

Here's a cardinal rule of anger: *all* angry behavior is driven by authentic need. It serves a function and a purpose. It may not be appropriate to the situation, it may be maladaptive, self-destructive, and downright dangerous, but it's authentic all the same. With consistent practice of presence and understanding skills, you will begin to see this rule as true for your teen. And there's a bonus: you will also begin to see the rule as true for *yourself*. That's a really worthwhile silver lining.

Let's begin to build this deeper seeing with a skill that brings us back to the basics of breath.

Skill Practice: Gap Breathing

When there's a moment of tension with your teen and it feels like the world's at stake, don't just prepare another point you want to make about your teen's behavior. Instead, use this breathing skill to connect you to what is most real for your teen *behind* the content of whatever you two are at odds about. Or, during a moment with your teen that is not immensely challenging but instead rather mundane, try the following:

1. Turn your attention away from what your teen is saying and doing. Instead, focus on your teen's breathing. See if you can notice the rise and fall of moment-to-moment breath. Start to track the rhythm of your teen's breath. The goal is to tune in to what's happening physically in that moment.

2. Listen through the gaps between your teen's words. Notice the small pauses and breaks in speech. The hesitations, the stops and starts, the ums and uhs.

3. Listen to the spaces. Can you hear the moments of meaning in your teen's tiny silences?

4. Notice what happens to your own awareness, thoughts, and responses after paying such close attention. How might your next action be more or less effective than if you'd simply waited and then jumped in with a more typical reaction? You don't need to do or say anything to your teen about this, and you need only do it for a few moments.

5. Note in your journal anything you have gleaned about what's most important from your teen's perspective. Return to the RSVP themes from chapter 1: respect, space, validation of feelings, and peers and provisions. Do your teen's bodily reactions suggest one of these things is at stake (at least from the teen's perspective)? Do they suggest your teen feels hurt, rejected, maligned, ignored, or like a failure in some way? Are you willing to get curious about the clues gestures and nonverbals can offer?

In the next practice, you'll deepen your understanding of what matters most to your teen—what's driving and fueling the anger. For this you'll need a blank piece of paper and an envelope.

Skill Practice: Sending and Receiving the Real Letter

1. Close your eyes and call your child to mind. Don't just think about your teen though—see your teen vividly in your mind's eye. How does your teen typically look? How does your teen sit, walk, and talk? What does your teen sound like? No judgments here, just visualize and notice. Once you have your teen vividly in mind, allow a recent difficult interaction to come to awareness, a time when communication broke down and anger flared. You might imagine it as a movie clip played in slow motion. Again, don't judge, just notice. Don't try to force the memory to surface. Let it come to mind in its own time.

2. Sit in a quiet place where you won't be disturbed for at least ten to fifteen minutes. On the envelope, write the specific external actions—the things you did or said—of this interaction. If you were angry that your teen didn't uphold an agreement, write out how you "used a sharp tone," or how you "lectured on how this has happened before," or that you "looked away and abruptly changed the topic." Whatever your actions were, list them. List them all, even if they include reactions you're now a bit ashamed of, such as swearing, yelling, accusing, or threatening. Write across the front and back of the envelope.

3. Next, taking the blank piece of paper, think about what deeper message you wanted your teen to receive. What was the intent behind the actions on the envelope? What was the feeling or need driving what you said? It might have a lot to do with worry or fear. Perhaps you were deeply concerned for your

teen's safety and future happiness and were trying to ensure your teen finally got on the right track. You'll likely find that these deeper messages relate to values of yours that have become blocked or stuck in some way. Whatever the deeper message, write out your best sense of these behind-your-behavior intentions and feelings.

4. Fold the letter, slip it into the envelope, and put it down.

5. Clear your mind. Center yourself with a minute of focusing on your breath. When you are ready, hold the envelope in your hands. Imagine that you are not you anymore—you are your teen. You have just received this letter in the mail. Read what's written across the envelope, all the actions and words hurled at "you." Read the words slowly and deliberately. To deepen the processing, you can even say them aloud if you like.

6. Sit for a moment with your eyes closed, feeling whatever arises as you imagine yourself as your teenager receiving this letter in the mail. What would be your impulse? What would you want to do with this envelope? Notice any thoughts or reactions that arise. It's a safe bet you're noticing little interest in what might be inside the envelope. You might even want to just toss the whole thing.

Has your teen been disregarding your letters—the true messages—because of the emotional and behavioral scrawls all over the envelope?

Skill Practice: Function Junction

In the previous practice, you likely got a visceral sense of why your teen misses your intended, valid messages. Now, let's take this a step further and help you connect with the true function of *your teen's* behavior. This practice helps you read the real letter inside even when the envelope makes you want to stamp it *return to sender*.

1. With a fresh envelope, do the same activity as above, but from your teen's perspective. What are your teen's observable behaviors—what does your teen *do*—when angry? Write these on the front and back of the envelope.

2. Next, on a fresh piece of paper, write your most compassionate, nonjudgmental guesses—think RSVP, think coercive cycles—about your teen's true message. What are your teen's unmet, blocked, or threatened needs? What values feel endangered to your teen?

3. If it feels appropriate, you can ask your teen to complete an envelope and letter. (If a family clinician is already involved, clinical assistance can be very helpful here.) Sometimes teens will be willing to write down not only the many angry things they do, but the authentic needs behind these behaviors as well.

4. If your teen does complete an envelope and letter, consider sharing your letters with each other. Such sharing can have a significant positive effect. However, only do so if you have put in the time and effort to practice the skills we've covered so far. You'll want to be able to slow down your body, recognize emotional patterning and rigid thinking, and mindfully maintain perspective. If you're not there yet, hold the letters until a later time. You *will* be ready soon.

The communication strategies in this book will help you connect with—though not necessarily agree with—your teen's perspective and needs. With their foundations in mindfulness and positive psychology, these strategies also help you to recognize the emotional and communication factors driving interactions and to respond skillfully and compassionately. As you practice, you will increasingly be able to help your teen—and yourself—move past the nastiness on the envelopes to the heartfelt letters inside.

The Courage of Compassionate Communication

Actor John Wayne got courage all wrong. His cinematic version of bravery portrayed it as a manly quality tied to an absence of fear and distress. As most of us know all too well, the toughest episodes overflow with fear and distress. True courage is doing what matters to release stuck patterns, despite the fear and distress and despite the pull of patterning.

To wrap up this chapter, let's explore a practice that can be used in any difficult moment. It's a simple process, but if practiced consistently, can have a profound effect.

Skill Practice: Hijacking the High Road

This practice can be used daily and is a way to begin practicing multiple skills that we've covered thus far in the book. When feeling stuck with your teen, do the following:

1. Establish yourself in presence with any of the mindfulness practices from chapter 2. Do so for at least several seconds.

2. Drawing on the Relational Compass, quickly notice any pull toward patterns of reactive closing that you may be experiencing.

3. Maintain presence. Imagine yourself resting in awareness at the very center of the Relational Compass.

4. Use mindfulness of thought—your BMW skills—to distance yourself from biased or distorted thinking.

5. Establish your understanding of what matters most in this moment. What needs or values are most pressing? What is behind your behavior? Your teen's behavior?

6. Ask yourself: *Am I willing to let go of my pattern and teach my teen the most valuable lesson I can right now?* Or, more simply: *Right now—will I open or close?*

If you can hijack moments of difficulty in this way, even just occasionally, you will be on your way to ending communication breakdowns.

Peaceful Parent Practice:
Hang Time with Your Teen

Parents who intentionally set aside time to connect with their children—including teens—and who work to modulate their emotional reactions are more likely to experience both improvements in the relationship and decreases in children's acting-out behavior (Kaminski, Valle, and Filene 2008; Obsuth et al. 2006). The following recommendations derive from a family intervention called Children Adult Relationship Enhancement, developed within a highly researched approach called Parent–Child Interaction Therapy (Chaffin et al. 2004). It's a set of guidelines for what to do and what to avoid during regular hang time with your teen.

When the relationship between a parent and teen is strained, the last thing a parent may feel inclined to do is spend precious free time hanging out with angry offspring. But that's exactly what this practice is asking of you. It is one of the most important practices in this book for shifting your relationship from conflict to connection.

1. Schedule at least ten (ideally fifteen or twenty) minutes daily to hang out with your teen, regardless of how difficult interactions have been. This is particularly hard to do when a day has included intensely upsetting exchanges. Do it anyway. Hang time is not a reward to be earned; it is relationship medicine dosed daily regardless of when things are challenging.

2. Let your teen choose an activity. Ideally, it's something inter-active, like a card or board game, but it may have to be an activity the teen is doing with you involved only as an observer, such as checking social media or playing an online game. It's crucial that you not dictate the activity.

3. Here's what you want to *do*:

    a. Praise your teen's effort and any behaviors during the interaction you can. Stretch if you have to, but avoid con-triving compliments. For example, you might say, "I like how you gave that a lot of thought," or, "I appreciate how real you can be with people," or, "Thanks for giving me a chance to try this."

    b. Paraphrase what your teen says, particularly the things that seem important to your teen. For example, "It sounds like you feel like that friend has it in for you."

    c. Point out what your teen is doing during the interaction so it's clear you are really paying attention. Point out, too, the things your teen is doing and saying that help the interac-tion flow smoothly. For example, "You're pausing to give me a chance to give my take on things," or, "Looks like you're switching to a different character in the game."

4. Here's what you want to *avoid*:

    a. Do not ask a lot of questions. If possible, do not ask any. Teens often perceive questions as being driven by an agenda—especially teens expecting conflict with parents. Leave questions alone no matter how tempted you are to pry or probe.

    b. Do not lead things or try to lecture. Hang time is *not* the time to teach anything. Swallow that impulse. Do not redirect your teen's behavior unless it becomes highly dis-ruptive or disrespectful. If this occurs, calmly tell your teen that you need to end the hang time for now—*and* that you're looking forward to next time.

Think of hang time as an investment. You're making a deposit during a down economy, on professional recommendation—mine and the literature's—that doing so will yield exponential dividends in the future. Keep showing up and giving your teen this specific, attuned attention. Even if your teen scoffs or shrugs you off, your perseverance will pay off.

Peaceful Parent Practice:
The Theater of the Mind

This chapter's additional Peaceful Parent Practice is a contemplation to return to regularly. The practice helps you achieve an emotional and mental altitude where perspective and understanding are more possible. While it's not an in-the-moment PURE practice, it can still do much to purify your intentions as a parent.

We go to the theater to see scripted interactions between characters. In our real, personal lives, we can do better. We don't have to follow our old scripts for our family patterns. We can improvise if we choose. Ask yourself: *Am I willing to create a new relationship with my experience of my child* right now? Your answer will determine whether the old pattern continues or if you take a new step forward. We can write new scripts for how we want to handle the emotions cropping up. As we do, others—especially our children—will notice us doing so. Even our small actions can have significant positive ripple effects.

Consider journaling for a few minutes. What old pattern—perhaps a coercive cycle—has recently surfaced in your parenting? As you write, note the thoughts, feelings, and even actions that rise up. Is it easy or difficult to stay with whatever your mind shares? If it's difficult, are you willing to stay with it anyway?

Consider again for a moment: Where did you learn your unworkable patterns? Where did your kids learn theirs? What about others in your life? What happens to your part of the pattern when you rest in skills of presence from chapter 2? When you rest in the skills of understanding from the current chapter? What will happen to the emotional inheritance you pass to your teen if you respond to your pattern in these ways?

Your Parental Agenda

As you move on to the next chapter:

☐ Continue your daily formal meditation practice.

☐ Continue your daily in-the-moment presence practices.

☐ Consult appendix A (available for download at http://www .newharbinger.com/35760) for more guidance on how to tailor practices of compassionate understanding to fit your needs.

☐ Begin and maintain daily hang time practice with your teen.

☐ Make going BMW with your thinking a daily habit. Build a wide angle lens to see the process of your thinking, particularly in the moments before, during, and after tough interactions.

☐ Use your journal for reflections and insights regarding this chapter's discussion of the Relational Compass, your own patterns of emotional reaction, and your experiences in working to create more emotional attunement with your teen.

4 Responsive Leadership in Parenting Angry Teens

The previous chapters built your basic mindfulness skills to improve your ability to handle difficult moments with your teen. You've worked to cultivate perspective-taking and to open yourself to compassion for what's happening emotionally behind the scenes, for both you and your teen. In this chapter, you'll get out of your head and heart and take action. This chapter focuses on leading teens toward new patterns—patterns that can transform suffering into possibility and connection.

In this chapter you will:

- Learn the power of sidestepping power struggles.

- Build skills for effective responses to angry behavior.

- Engage in practices designed to increase your energy and resilience.

- Learn how to set limits on behavior and manage crises while maintaining composure and compassion.

Seeing Beyond Power Moves and Pitched Battles

When I was a child, I loved to toss rocks into the large reservoir down the street from my house. Sometimes I skipped them on the surface. When thin, flat rocks were unavailable, I opted for big chunky ones that would make the biggest *kerplunk*! I loved to stand and watch the water ripple out from the point of impact. As parents, we all hope to trigger such rippling. We hope for a positive impact that will carry forward in our children's lives—and through them into the lives of others we may never meet.

Researchers Nicholas Christakis and James Fowler (2011) have documented contagion in moods and behaviors within social networks. Simply by being in relationship with others, by being associated with others, peoples' likelihood for experiencing significant mood states such as loneliness and depression, as well as problem behaviors such as smoking and overeating, increases dramatically. Moods and behaviors appear to be contagious—or, to put it another way, they can ripple out among people.

The current thinking is that our basic social natures lead us to constantly and automatically process emotional information about the people we encounter. We observe each other's facial expressions, gestures, tones, and emotional tendencies. And, without intending to, we subtly mimic one another, sparking emotion and behavior.

We are contagious to our children—and they to us—whether we intend it or not. While more research on mood contagion remains to be done, what we know already poses important questions for parents: What sort of infectious agent do you want to be for your kids? What specific emotions and perspectives do you hope to spread?

When we get caught up in pointless games of tug-of-war with our teens, we miss opportunities to coach them to manage emotion effectively. What is more important in these moments—being right or being a good mentor? Caregivers—clinicians like me and parents like you—need to step out of reaction and cultivate proactive responses. You can't create positive ripples if you're wasting time yanking at ropes by the water's edge.

Ask Abblett

Q: My teen seems to be doing a lot of frustrating things on purpose. Aren't they sometimes just trying to provoke a fight with me?

A: Yes, your teen is indeed intentionally doing frustrating things in heated moments with you and others. And yes, your teen is looking to get a rise out of you at times. But also no—your teen isn't angry or lashing out due to any sort of master plan. Your teen's overall cycle of emotions and behavior is out of their control.

When we focus on concepts of power or control in parenting an angry teen, we tend to neglect truly understanding the teen's behavior struggles. As we discussed in chapter 3, it's important to understand what's going on behind the behavior and to recognize any RSVP needs that have either gone unmet or are perceived as threatened.

As a therapist, I once tried to leverage a teen client into owning up to a serious abusive behavior he'd done in his past. In an earlier session, this client had disclosed some significant family-related pain. I made the error of trying to impress my superiors by using that information to get this teen to fess up. Not only did he not do so, he completely shut down on therapy. I was then faced with the crisis of my own accountability. I had to either own my error and take a *one-down* stance (more on that in a moment) with this teen, or stubbornly cling to my justifications.

A talented supervisor nudged me in the right direction: "That kid had the guts to be real with you. I wonder if you should be real with him."

So I let go of being the high and mighty therapist and let myself be a human being. I told the teen I'd screwed up, and that I would understand if he wanted a new therapist. I put the ball in his court. Thankfully, he hit it back to me. We kept working together. He made great strides in treatment, and I learned a great deal about the power of authenticity. Much of this applies to parenting an angry teen as well.

Taking a one-down stance involves owning your piece of the coercive cycle of anger and disconnection. It's the opposite of one upping. Rather than increase your attack, you let down your guard. In the next practice we explore how to actually do this.

Skill Practice: Letting Down Your Guard with a One-Upping Teen

With this practice, you work to make a habit of authenticity when you feel tempted to insist on being right or engage in tug-of-war with your teen. This practice is both a contemplation to do in quiet moments as well as an active practice to use with your teen.

1. Sitting quietly, consider a time in your life when an adult, particularly a family member, took personal responsibility—without an excess of self-loathing—for a misstep that hurt others. Take a moment. Notice how you regard this person *now* for having done that *then*. This is the message you want to communicate to your teen. This will teach accountability better than any lecture will, particularly if you model it.

2. Contemplate a recent example of tug-of-war with your teen. Focus on a moment where you refused to bend, even though you had clearly been in the wrong in some way—even if that was only in how you spoke. Visualize in detail replacing this rigidity with a one-down stance. What would it look and feel like to replace these behaviors with an openness and willingness to be wrong? Notice how this feels. How might your teen regard this choice—and you—twenty years from now? What message will you have sent?

3. In the midst of an ongoing episode, look for the moment to be a responsive leader of the relationship with your teen. It will be just after you've crossed a line—when you're clinging to correctness or lost in a rant. Or perhaps you've simply dismissed your teen and walked away in a huff. Regardless, first, take a breath—cultivate presence—and remember and understand the RSVP behind your teen's anger.

4. Now, respond. Say something like:

    "Hey, I know I've gone too far. I apologize for yelling."

"Sorry for cutting you off. I know I don't like it when people do that to me."

"I may disagree with what you did, but that doesn't give me the right to judge you or reject everything you have to say. I'm sorry for that."

Giving Leeway

Consider how many years, billions of dollars, and lives were wasted during the nuclear arms race between the United States and the Soviet Union. And now, by contrast, consider the stance that Mahatma Gandhi took with the British Empire. What was different in Gandhi's approach to conflict versus how the United States approached conflict with the Soviets?

Gandhi acted in the direction of connection, of relationship. He did not look to force separation or leverage violent control. Rather, he sought compassionate, inevitable change. When summarizing his non-violent philosophy of "satyagraha," Gandhi (2001) suggested that change amidst conflict comes by appealing to the reason and conscience of one's opponent. It is perspective, the ability to assume the healing role—to maintain compassion—that makes progression toward victory possible.

This is the stance of a responsive leader. As a parent, you may never approach Gandhi's level of equanimity and perseverance, but you can build a peace-conducive platform for your daily interactions. You can offer compassion, see what's truly behind your teen's anger, and show respect for your teen's highest self. The following practice helps you build such a platform.

Skill Practice: Lending-a-Hand Meditation

A few simple questions can help you put a new frame on your difficult exchanges with your teen. Choose one or more of the following questions and post it somewhere around the house where you'll see it regularly. These are your prompts for a wider, more compassionate perspective on your child's behavior.

What am I missing here?

How else could I view this?

What am I assuming about the other person?

What else is causing this?

An attitude of curiosity about how you might shift your relationship into a new, more productive space can go a long way. If you can remember to pause and ask yourself such questions before you react (this is difficult!), you have a chance to sidestep your old scripts and respond with compassion.

1. Based on an honest answer in a given situation, imagine holding out a hand to your teen in a gesture of offering. Let go of your agenda, your need for control or to be right. In your mind's eye, see yourself reaching out.

2. Now, in actuality, say or do something as an act of giving. Offer a sincere—not sarcastic, not lecturing—wish. Speak to what your teen most wants. Talk about how you hope your teen can get this need met in a healthy way. Offer to help. Offer to make your teen a sandwich. Whatever you come up with, make this moment an opportunity to model the power of nonreactive giving.

And Yet Standing Your Ground

Your teen expects you to do your typical back and forth—the lecturing, demanding, arguing, and escalation of the coercive cycle. You want to break that cycle. You want to step away from escalation and unresolved anger and toward compassion, connection, and effective resolution (also known as a happier kid and parent!).

When taking a one-down stance, you need to lower your guard. But that's not the same as caving in. You're not a doormat to walk on. You're not a target in search of arrows. And although you're not reacting or escalating, you *are* sending a message of solidity and certainty.

Here's the basic emotional message you want to begin to send your teen as regularly and consistently as possible: *I'm here, I am working to hang in this with you because our relationship matters to me, and you're neither bad nor wrong for having the experience you're having.* We can abbreviate this to the mantra "Here, now, you matter."

It's not about saying this mantra aloud. (That would certainly serve as conclusive evidence to your teen of your adult awkwardness!) It's the *how* of your stance. Your new, connected dance step with your teen comes from how you embody these words in your emotions and behavior. So let's practice the physical manifestation of this stance.

Skill Practice: Grounding Breaths

Famous mindfulness teacher Thich Nhat Hanh has said that we should "walk as if we are kissing the Earth with our feet" (1999, 28). What he means is that when we cultivate presence we begin to really feel the ground and become connected with it. Let's practice how to be both light and grounded, so that we are no longer blown around by the stress of anger.

1. Stand tall and erect but not rigid.

2. Close your eyes and take a slow, deep, centering breath.

3. Continue breathing slowly and deeply. As you breathe in, imagine the air going all the way down through your body, all the way to your feet.

4. Continue breathing this way, allowing the breath to continue down through your body until you can feel the sensations of your feet against the floor.

5. If your mind becomes distracted or sensations arise elsewhere in your body, just gently return to this breathing down into and through your feet. Really let yourself feel the sensations there.

6. Imagine your body becoming light and clear as the air moves down through it.

7. Imagine your feet becoming firmly in contact with the ground.

8. Continue breathing. Know that you are light, clear, and grounded where you are.

Now, try practicing this in a more everyday fashion: while at home—even in the midst of interactions with your teen—simply pause and breathe lightness of body and solidity of stance into the moment you're in. Do you think others, including your offspring, can notice any shift in you when you do so? What message does that send?

Confidence Amidst Chaos

In the *Tao Te Ching*, the classic text from the sixth century, Lao Tzu declares, "The sage acts by doing nothing, teaches without speaking, attends all things without making claim on them" (2012, 145). What Lao Tzu refers to here is the ancient principle of *wu-wei*, the power of change that comes from not trying to force change to happen.

Remember, trees may be firmly rooted to the ground, but they are more flexible and have give at the top. There's a *wu-wei* to assuming such a stance. The wind will blow, and, yes, it will shove at you. But you won't meet it—your teen's emotions—with rigid resistance. You'll let the surge of your teen's angst push through, and yet you won't be going anywhere. Your teen's anger will not uproot and topple you, as it would that inflexible oak of an old-school grandparent who insists your teen is in need of tough love.

Recent research on the concept of *grit*, or perseverance and emotional commitment to long-term goals, is relevant here. Researchers such as Angela Duckworth at the University of Pennsylvania have pre-sented data showing that students with higher grit scores were signifi-cantly more likely to advance in their educations, have higher GPAs, and even rank higher in the National Spelling Bee (Duckworth et al. 2007). Grit was predictive of these outcomes over and above intelligence and other aspects of personality. This unwavering commitment is clearly something we want for our children. It starts with our grit as parents, by which I mean the willingness and skill to lead your angry teen.

As W. H. Murray wrote in *The Scottish Himalaya Expedition*, "Concerning all acts of initiative (and creation), there is one elemen-tary truth, the ignorance of which kills countless ideas and splendid plans: that the moment one definitely commits oneself, then Providence moves too… A whole stream of events issues from the decision, raising in one's favor all manner of unforeseen incidents, meetings and mate-rial assistance" (1951, 6–7). Parenting an angry teen requires no less grit than does trekking the Himalayas. The results that come from the commitment to practice the skills in this book—despite the discom-fort, pain, and outright angst of doing so—open up possibilities for choice and connection that would not otherwise have arisen.

In my early twenties, I dropped out of law school. This wasn't due to intellectual weakness or lack of desire. I left due to insufficient grit. I didn't have a honed, practiced skill set for committed action. (By the way, Duckworth's data also suggests that grit can predict fewer career changes.) I almost dropped out of my graduate training in psychology as well. Thankfully, by that point, I'd started to learn a bit about per-severance that has helped me tremendously in my roles as clinician, author, and, yes, parent. Let's turn now to a daily practice of grit.

Skill Practice: GRIT Without Grinding Yourself Up

This practice is important to practice both narrowly (around your par-enting) and broadly (in your daily life more generally). Choose an endeavor that can drain, fatigue, or vex you but is nonetheless important. Maybe it's helping your irritable adolescent with homework. Maybe it's leaning into the neglected household budget or financial plan. Regardless, try the following steps. Use a journal to record your thoughts and self-assessment.

1. Go to, or at least visualize, the space or context where you're intending to get something unpleasant yet necessary done. Notice any impulse to withdraw, distract, or rush through it. Ask yourself, is the **G***rass* actually any greener elsewhere? Will other grass actually be free of all difficulties similar to what you're experiencing now? What will the cost be, to you or others, if you go after that greener pasture? What pattern will this create? What message will it send to others? To your teen in particular? Sit in awareness of what shows up in your thoughts, images, and sensations. Just notice what arises.

2. **R***ecommit* to the course that matters, the course that is most consistent with the needs of your teen, you, and the whole family. If your epitaph were to one day reflect this decision, what would you have it read?

3. Make a clear **I**ntention to enact a first, concrete action step toward that course. Notice what happens in mind and body when you sincerely do so.

4. **T***ake* a leap and take that concrete action *now*.

Remember: to lead your teen away from anger, you need to send a message of compassionate roots-in-the-ground certainty. And grit isn't inconsistent with the *wu-wei* stance of nonaction. Rather, the two concepts balance and fuel each other. The best persistence (grit) comes without resistance (*wu-wei*). You've probably heard "what you resist persists" before. Here, we're flipping that on its head. You'll best hang in there with your teen's difficulties—and be most helpful—if you do so with flexibility and flow rather than tension or a grinding force of will.

Ask Abblett

Q: How am I supposed to hold on to a sense of hope when I've been dealing with this problem with my kid for so long? When nothing ever seems to fix things?

A: While it can indeed continue to be painful and difficult, it may be important to ask yourself a different question: *If it's painful right now and my thoughts are telling me to give up or give in, what's the most important response for me to make despite the pain? Am I willing to do so regardless of what may or may not come down the line?*

Fueling Yourself for Action

Before going further into how you can compassionately manage your teen's anger-related behavior, let's pause to explore another practice. This breathing activity can help you build the energy and emotional fuel to do the work of compassionate yet direct management of problem behavior.

Skill Practice: Fire Breathing

1. With your eyes closed, sit upright without being tense or rigid.

2. Begin to breathe as fully and deeply into the belly as possible, with the breath expanding the belly on the inhale.

3. Don't allow the typical pause between inhale and exhale. Instead, keep the breath flowing with energy and motion, like your abdomen is a bellows feeding a fire.

4. Continue to breathe in this deep, powerful way for a count of at least thirty cycles of inhale and exhale.

5. Consider adding a mantra, to be said aloud or to yourself, with the cadence of the breath. For example, "listen" (inhale),

"now" (exhale), "look" (inhale), "now" (exhale), "leap" (inhale), "now" (exhale). Adding this mantra can help galvanize the energy created by your deep breathing to support the actions you need to take as a parent.

On Target in Managing Your Teen's Behavior

As a clinician, I've heard both parents and professionals express concern regarding behavior management strategies that call for parents to assert authority over kids' behavior. Call it limit-setting, behavioral consequences, whatever: for many it calls up images of angry spankings and punitive angst. And of course reactive, intense punishment of behavior is not only ineffective—it can make things worse for an angry teen. But this doesn't mean that teens do not need limits placed on their behavior. This doesn't mean that if we just nurture them and praise them enough, eventually the negative behaviors will fall away.

In my twenty years of experience with angry youth, such an approach fails in two respects. First, it doesn't help teens learn the cause-and-effect relationship of their angry behaviors on others, thereby muddling their development of healthy self-responsibility. Second, it distorts families' relationship patterns, such that teens get the message that anger is the ticket to desired ends. A purely nurturing, empathic communication approach—that is, one without compassionately set limits on behavior—also sends teens the message that the world cannot help shift this unrest in their minds and bodies, that it is uncontrollable. These are not healthy messages for teens to internalize and carry into their own years of parenting.

Yes, kids need compassion and empathy. Yes, we need to take their perspectives, needs, and dearth of necessary skills into account. But in order to help them feel safe, in order to create a foundation for building skills and self-responsibility, caregivers must be willing to erect compassionate fences around angry, acting-out behavior.

Such actions may provoke significant fear, anxiety, and frustration in parents, particularly when there's been a long history of not setting boundaries. However, when presence and compassionate understanding are wedded to setting boundaries and establishing consequences, teens learn to trust that their chaos *can* be contained. Research indicates that youth who perceive containment strategies in the parenting they receive are significantly less likely to exhibit aggressive behavior than those who do not believe their parents are willing or able to contain them (Schneider, Cavell, and Hughes 2003). These "contained" kids receive messages of willingness and engagement from their parents. They receive a healthy dose of consistency and predictability. They experience the safety and security of their attachment with their parents. All of this creates fertile ground for teens to learn how to manage their behavior in new, more productive ways.

You know from your own experience that households descend into chaos without such boundaries. However, if we're not mindful while erecting boundaries, they can end up being far more reactive than necessary. Ideally, such boundaries should feel like compassionate guiding hands. To teens especially, though, such boundaries can feel much more like hammers.

What we're aiming for here is a stance of calm, self-assured strength. Returning to Gandhi, his calm strength yielded acts of courage and compassion, including his famous fasts to protest British policies in India and his gestures of compassion toward angry protestors and followers alike.

Of course, you're not Mahatma Gandhi. But you do have a deep emotional investment in your teen. You are willing to attempt to lead your relationship out of the angry chaos. There was nothing supernatural about Gandhi. Rather, he drew on the power of presence and compassionate communication. If you didn't possess the potential for these skills, you wouldn't have made it this far in this book.

Speaking the Truth to Your Teen

You want your teen to listen, to just once actually do what you're asking without the grumbling, disrespect, or outright hostility. And your teen wants you to stop nagging, to understand that what your teen is doing at the moment is important. Think back to the coercive cycle from chapter 1, where the dad objects to the teen's laundry-strewn room while the teen taps at his phone. (If you need a reminder, perhaps revisit the related "Parent-Teen Coercive Cycle" graphics.)

"Oh, my god! Stop with the damn nagging! I heard you the first time. I'll do it when I'm done with this text! God!" Sound familiar? Notice how simply reading this sparks thoughts and sensations in your body. Recall the skills of mindful presence you learned in chapter 2. And while you're at it, remember, too, to look behind you teen's angry words, to get curious about how that texting might indeed be crucial from your teen's perspective. Let your thoughts of *rightness* pass by.

You're ready now to give a directive if necessary—perhaps a medication needs to be taken, or attendance at a family event is required, or pungent trash heaped in a bedroom corner really must be cleared. However, there's still another skill you need before you step into your teen's bedroom, interrupt the texting, and issue your well-justified directive.

To break the destructive pattern of interaction between you and your teen, you need to learn to deliver concise, direct, and nonreactive directions. The following four-step series of skill practices helps you learn this skill:

Skill Practice: Speaking Behind Behavior (Step 1)

First, please revisit chapter 1 to review the needs behind your teen's angry behavior toward authority figures. Remember, angry teens are sending authentic RSVP messages, but these are often obscured by angry, volatile behavior. Your job as a parent is to get to that real message—and to let your teen know you're sincere in your attempt to understand. You're not looking to manipulate or spin things. You genuinely want to learn and respond to what is truly important to your child.

This skill takes a significant amount of practice to get the hang of it. Are you willing? What is the cost of continuing with patterns as they are?

1. Anchor yourself in your breathing. Feel the breath in your body as you inhale and exhale one complete breath.

2. Notice something in your immediate surroundings or bodily sensations. Quickly and silently, notice something that is here and now separate from what your mind may be saying about your teen.

3. Consider what RSVP need may be behind your teen's current unpleasant, angry, or disrespectful behavior. What aspect is most important to your teen in this moment? Respect, space, validation of feelings, or perhaps peers and provisions?

4. Notice any blankness, pushback, or "but" reactions in your mind. Let them pass. Hold on to the need behind your teen's nasty behavior.

5. Now, look at your teen as calmly and directly as possible and say, "I can see that it's very important to you that _____ [insert what's behind your teen's behavior]." For example, "I can see that there must be something really important you're texting to someone and that you want to make sure you connect with them about it right now."

6. Wait and really watch your teen's physical response to what you've said. Does your teen's posture open, stay the same, or tighten or otherwise suggest increased anger? If it's at least stayed the same, continue. If not, if your teen continues to shut down or attack, say that you want to discuss this further and that you hope you both can learn to resolve these bad patterns rather than simply repeat them. Explain that it's not helpful to

continue the conversation right now and then make your exit. Do so without nonverbal expressions of angst, frustration, or dejection.

7. If your teen seems to be opening and softening, continue to express yourself. Notice the bodily sensations showing up for you in this situation. Can you share these with your teen? Doing so models openness and the crucial skill of getting out of the head (thinking) and into the heart of felt experience (the pattern of sensations we call an emotion). For example, "Right now, I'm noticing a clenching in my stomach and heat around my face. I'm stressed and frustrated."

8. Next say, "It's important to me that _____ [insert an issue or activity you consider crucial]." For example, "It's important to me that you and I have a quick chat about something. I would appreciate it if we could do that as soon as you finish sending that text."

9. Again, wait and really watch. Acknowledge and authentically reinforce any effort your teen makes to engage with you.

Skill Practice: Giving Effective Directions (Step 2)

Adapted from Chorpita and Weisz's MATCH-ADTC protocol (2009)

Your teen has looked away from the phone and looks at you.

1. Notice and let go of the dismissive furrows on your teen's face. Bring mindful presence and continued attention to the need behind your teen's behavior.

2. Use a direct yet positive tone. Maintain eye contact without glaring. If your teen is sitting, try sitting or otherwise mirroring your teen before you speak.

3. Remember *wu-wei*: let go of controlling the outcome. Your only goal is to deliver an effective direction with presence and compassion. The fact that your teen may not comply is not your focus. Your focus is on you and effective delivery. Outcomes will simply come.

4. Whatever the direction is, make sure you break it down into clear, specific steps. Don't simply say, "Clean your room"; rather, start with a specific direction such as, "Please put the dirty clothes on the floor into the hamper."

5. State the direction calmly, directly, and with a neutral tone. Don't ask your teen. This isn't a question. Avoid question phrases like, "Will you...?" or, "Might you...?" or, "Do you think you could be so kind...?" Research shows that questions often yield noncompliance. An effective direction is a polite, direct *statement*. For example, "Please pick up your dirty clothes from the floor and place them in the hamper."

6. Do *not* immediately repeat the direction. Give your teen a moment. If there is no response, repeat the direction using the same phrasing. Do *not* show frustration or irritation through eye rolling, sighing, or the like. This will only escalate the coercive cycle.

7. If your teen still doesn't respond, simply exit the situation without engaging your teen further. Avoid pleading, nagging, threats, and guilt trips. Hold yourself in presence and know that you've done excellent work in practicing mindful parent management skills. That itself is a victory.

Attuning to Your Teen By Tuning Out

I once had a client who was a former Catholic priest. This former priest had adopted his daughter when she was three. The daughter had

had a very difficult early childhood prior to her adoption; as a teen, she struggled to trust that her relationships could be lasting, safe, and supportive—especially her relationship with her dad.

Coercive cycles would frequently erupt between them. And when they did, the teen would get in her dad's face and swear and yell. "I hate you. I wish you'd die!"

This father was wired on the anxious side. For him, emotional intensity sparked patterns of withdrawal and avoidance.

"And you're a goddamn bastard!" the daughter would yell at glass-shattering pitch.

Remember, this was a former priest. Swearing alone was bad enough, but "bastard" was off the charts. "That's it," the dad would yell back. "I'm sending you to a residential program before your anger kills me with a heart attack!"

You can imagine what this self-defensive push from the dad did to the teen's deep-seated fears of neglect and rejection. Things continued to grow more strained and more painful between them.

In a parenting session, I asked the dad to say "the b-word" aloud, just as his teen had done. He protested. I insisted. Sheepishly he said it. I asked him to say it again, to keep repeating it as fast as he could. I promised I'd do it with him.

When we finally stopped, I asked what he had noticed about the word, about what had happened to the sound and feel of it.

"The word lost its meaning. It became nonsense," he said.

And that was the point. The message wasn't that this parent should simply permit disrespectful language to be slung in his direction. He shouldn't be a doormat for his teen's anger. The point was for him to see "bastard" as merely a word—to deliteralize it so he could ignore both its meaning and the provocations from his teen. When he mindfully ignored words that stung, he could focus instead on leading and managing the difficult situation.

Now, returning to our practice, let's assume you've delivered a great, efficient direction for your teen's behavior. Nonetheless, your teen is lashing out at you. Here's step three in the management process:

Skill Practice: Selective Attending: Leaning In While Tuning Out (Step 3)

I grew up watching and reading *Peanuts* cartoons. As a kid, I didn't really understand the point of the teacher's *wah wah wah wah* broken-record talking. As an adult—and particularly an adult who has spent years trying to get kids to listen—I get it. Kids can tune adults out. Adults can too. In fact, active ignoring can be a productive skill for you to practice as a parent when your teen is ranting and you're working to sidestep reactivity and lead the interaction on to a healthy path. Here are the steps:

1.   With your journal, notebook, or tablet, spend a few minutes brainstorming the specific words your teen has used that most upset you. Don't hold back. List the unpleasant, the downright nasty—whatever words punch you in the gut. Whether they are words used to describe you, your teen, others, or your teen's world, list the words that have caused you significant pain.

2.   Next, as in the preceding example, take a word and say it aloud, perhaps even in the tone your teen uses. Notice the reactions in your mind and body. You just ran your internal Geiger counter over a radioactive word. Did the meter jump? Use your presence skills to bear witness to the changes that arise with this spoken word.

3.   Say the word aloud, over and over and as fast as you can. What do you notice about your experience of this word? Does the meter jump as much as it did before?

4.   Imagine yourself in an upcoming interaction with your teen in which that word is fired at you. See yourself there in the room. Vividly see and hear your teen in your imagination. Say the word over and over quietly in your mind while you watch the rant unfold.

5. Attend less to your teen and more to what is happening within your own experience. When you practice active ignoring, do your emotions surge as they normally do? Does your body clench? If not, what does this suggest about your ability to manage the situation with greater flexibility?

6. Create an inventory of all the trigger words and phrases your teen uses that push your buttons. Commit to a practice of active ignoring for all of them.

It's important to be aware here of what we in the field call *extinction bursts*. When someone is used to consistently receiving a certain rewarding reaction to a behavior and you eliminate that reaction, the person will, for a time, actually *increase* the frequency and intensity of the behavior. So, for example, if you're actively ignoring the "b-word," your teen may escalate its use. This is actually a good sign. It means that your teen was getting a reward from your reactions to the word, and is now working hard—mostly subconsciously—to get that reward back.

This is where you double down and stay consistent. Continue your active ignoring, continue your practice of presence and understanding. If you don't give the reward of your reaction, the behavior will decrease and fall away. And if you hang in there long enough, you will also be rewarded yourself by the feeling of empowerment that comes from helping shift these entrenched patterns. It is possible!

Skill Practice: Compassionate Consequences (Step 4)

Let's return to our scenario. You've engaged thoughtfully and genuinely. You've given an effective, concise direction. You've practiced active ignoring. But now your teen is trashing the living room.

You've already made it clear that destructive behavior would result in a loss of privileges. No cell phone use and no hanging out with friends over the weekend. It's clear your teen crossed a line. Though you dread the uproar to come, you also know it's time for you to follow through—not doing so would erode your credibility and decrease your influence.

Step 4 helps you strike a balance between containment and compassion:

1. *Get calm:* Check your presence. Are you mindfully monitoring your senses? Do *not* follow the surge of your own anger to swoop up behind an angry, out-of-control teen in order to put a consequence in place. Only state a limit from a place of relative calm, flexibility, and leadership. Avoid acting from reactivity and constriction. You don't have to "win" by dropping a consequence hammer on an already raging teen. A limit is still effective when you follow up on it a bit later.

2. *Get clear internally:* Before stating and enforcing a limit, step up your understanding. Are you taking a healthy perspective? Are you seeing behind your teen's behavior to the RSVP needs driving it? Even though your teen needs to learn accountability for the problematic behavior, you can still rest in compassion for the needs nudging the teen to act out. Be mindful of how emotional reactions are showing up as sensations in your body. Can you identify exactly where you feel these reactions (for example, heat, rigidity, clenching) and what they feel like?

3. *Get clear externally:* Explain specifically which behavior is inappropriate and why. (Perhaps it can hurt or offend others, or it's unsafe, or disrespectful.) Say something concise, such as, "You kicked the bathroom door and broke it. Breaking things like that could lead to either you or someone else getting hurt."

4. *State the consequence:* Don't explain it. Don't apologize for it. Just calmly and concisely say it: "Because you broke the door

in anger, you're losing your cell phone privilege, you won't be allowed to leave the house tonight, and you'll need to pay for replacement items out of your savings account."

5. *Be reasonable*: Make sure the consequence is focused on helping your teen learn a boundary, not on reactively punishing. Offer alternatives for how your teen can behave in the future. "Next time, instead of swearing at me and shutting down, if you leave me a note asking if I can take you to the mall, I will make sure to respond to you."

6. *Be consistent*: Be sure to follow through. If your teen responds appropriately, offer kudos or caring assistance. If your teen does not, follow through on the consequences. This is the step that is often problematic for parents. As we've discussed, anger is often a protective layer for fear and uncertainty. When you follow through, you make things more certain—and this goes a long way to help teens get on top of their anger.

Remember, good limits are done with your teen's underlying needs in mind. They are compassionate fences meant to create a space within which teens can feel safe and supported as you help them modify their behavior.

Being the Calm: Co-Regulation Skills for Managing Behavior

Let's back up a bit. Instead of addressing your teen's angry behavior only after it has escalated, what if you could intervene earlier in the process to shift your teen toward a calmer state? There's a deer-in-headlights aspect to others' anger, particularly if you've been there many times before with this particular loved one. But you don't have to passively watch your teen build toward full-blown rage.

The challenge is to abide the anxiety, apprehension, and fear you'll experience with mindfulness—and to move toward your teen anyway. Then you can interrupt the angry script and nudge the interaction toward a *co-regulation activity*, a physical or mental activity that calls for mutual give and take.

Instead of just arguing with a teen's disrespectful grumbling, you could try picking up a small, soft ball and tossing it gently in their direction. It's a rare kid who will let a ball approach without trying to catch it. You then silently raise your hands in full expectation that your teen will toss—hopefully not hurl—it back to you. The point is to begin a coordinated flow back and forth between you. This could involve playing catch, spinning a quarter to and fro across the dining room table, or maybe even placing a trash can between you and taking turns tossing in balled-up paper. The point is to create a resonance between you, a shared rhythm that pulls your teen out of the angry ruminating and gets your teen's mind and body coordinating with yours. This is co-regulation. It's a skill that requires a combination of playfulness, courage, and timing. These are qualities that, as a parent of an angry teen, you have undoubtedly demonstrated at some point. Are you willing to call upon them now to teach your teen that angry ranting need not be inevitable? Help your kid learn that it's possible to break the buildup.

Co-regulation activities have double impact. One, Co-regulation activities physically and mentally disrupt escalation patterns. And two, co-regulation activities also send teens a clear message of your caring and willing engagement.

The following are the key steps to any co-regulation activity:

Skill Practice: Offering Co-Regulation M&Ms

1. As we practiced in chapter 3, remember to see your teen's moody grumbling as a **M**essage, an emotional indicator of a perceived threat or an unmet need.

2. **Mo**ve in support of your teen. Don't ask, "Hey, would you like to do a co-regulation activity with me like my parenting book suggests?" Instead, just pick up a ball—or whatever is on hand—and move toward your teen.

3. **Me**et the need. As you engage in your back-and-forth playful activity, express a sincere desire to help your teen take care of the inner tension that led to the reactivity in the first place. For example, while tossing a ball back and forth, you might say, "Hey, I want you to know that I'm not going anywhere. I shifted my schedule so that I could be available to help you with that project. But only if you want my help."

4. **Mo**ld your teen toward self-regulation. As you do the back and forth of the activity, aim for a rhythm—almost as if you're dancing. See if you can slow the cadence of the activity. See if your teen can take the lead and set the pace. Let your teen's emotional system get what it needs out of the activity—while still feeling safe.

5. **Me**ssage, in a brief, teen-friendly way, that you really appreciate the teen's effort to downshift the intensity of things with you. Explain that this matters to you and that you respect your teen's willingness to do so. With teens, sometimes this is best accomplished through a knowing gesture, such as a fist bump or similar, and a few quick words.

Building Your Teen's Problem-Solving Skills

Research definitively shows that developing clearer and more consistent problem-solving skills can help kids who struggle with anger to sidestep the ladder of escalation and instead actually address the obstacles that face them (Barkley and Robin 2013).

Anger makes solving problems more difficult because anger activates brain pathways that make the planning and thinking centers of the prefrontal cerebral cortex less effective. Anger narrows people's ability to achieve perspective and facilitates erroneous perceptions (such as the correspondence bias with its blaming tendency that we discussed in chapter 3).

Parents can help teens manage their anger by directly modeling, teaching, and guiding teens to practice discrete problem-solving skills. With consistent practice—which requires modeling—angry reactivity can gradually be replaced by an investigatory approach to resolving life dramas. In turn, the success of using such problem-solving skills reinforces the skills. And once teens see how much these skills improve their lives, the skills become self-maintaining.

Skill Practice: Teach Them To SOLVE Problems

Adapted from Chorpita and Weisz's MATCH-ADTC protocol (2009)

Stop: practice mindfulness to sidestep reactive thoughts and ride out agitation in the body.

Observe what's happening objectively and with a focus on facts rather than judgments or labels.

List all possible solutions—including positive ones and negative ones—you can think of.

Verify what might work by putting an option into action.

Examine the factual results and try another option if necessary.

Holding the Line with Unsafe Behavior

Sometimes parents cannot—and should not—try to manage their teen's angry behavior all on their own. I have worked with far too many families in which unsafe aggressive and destructive behavior has become the norm and parents and kids live in fear of the next escalation. Whole families can become paralyzed by such fear, trapped in patterns that are unhealthy for everyone.

For teens to improve, it is absolutely crucial to send them a message of adult leadership and containment. You want it emblazoned in your teen's mind—even when anger structures in the brain partially blind your teen—that you *will* take action to keep everyone safe in the home. A number of fears and doubts can make parents reluctant to send this message or follow it with appropriate action. Here are just a few:

My teen will get more angry and dangerous if I hold the line.

My teen will never forgive me for the betrayal.

I know my teen will never *actually* hurt us. It's just bluster.

I can't have police and emergency personnel rolling up to my house and creating a scene in front of all our neighbors.

Calling a crisis team to come to our house will mean I've completely failed as a parent.

There may be others as well, but you get the gist. These sentiments, though understandable, are obstacles to be overcome. Without a clear safety plan, the risks of dangerous situations worsen. Further, failure to create and use a safety plan can damage relationships between family members. Siblings may resent that you cave in and don't take action, while your angry teen will further learn how powerful anger can be in swaying the course of things. You trap yourself in a vortex of fear and hopelessness.

If physically aggressive or destructive behavior—or frequent threats of it—are present, it's important to create a safety plan. When creating this plan, a licensed clinician with experience working with risk behaviors in families can be very helpful.

Ask Abblett

Q: People tell me that I shouldn't tolerate my kid's unsafe behavior at home—that I should be calling the cops or at least taking him to the emergency room for a psychiatric screening. But I know he's not really going to hurt anyone. Isn't it true that calling 911 can just make things worse?

A: Yes and no. Yes, there's an element of uncertainty when you call in authorities to intervene. There's no guarantee that they'll be sensitive to the clinical factors causing the outbursts—or even that they won't arrest him. Likewise, there's no guarantee that it won't just end up an exciting story for him to share at school.

And no—involving external authorities can be a crucial step in breaking the pattern of toxic behavior in the home. There is much you can do to pave the way for a better response from emergency personnel or a specialized community-based crisis team, and to start giving your teen a clear, consistent message that there is a line that cannot be crossed without you taking action.

Skill Practice: Matter-of-Fact Safety Planning

As we've discussed, teens can't learn to manage their volatile emotions if they don't feel safe. Teens need to feel that caregivers are there to make sure things don't spiral too far out of control. That's why a collaboratively created home safety plan is crucial. "Collaborative" is the key word here. The teen should have the opportunity to contribute to the creation of the plan. Even if the offer to collaborate is rebuffed, the respectful and compassionate message this conveys is crucial. A safety planning worksheet is available online for you to download; visit http://www.newharbinger.com/35760 to access it. Here are the essential steps:

1. Identify the outcomes desired from the safety plan from the perspective of all parties.

2. Be specific about the safety-related behaviors that your teen needs to avoid. Be sure there are no judgments in the labeling of these behaviors. Keep your words descriptive.

3. List any red flags or triggering factors—in the environment or people's behavior—that tend to occur *immediately prior* to unsafe behaviors.

4. List any early-warning situational variables or behaviors that indicate things are heading toward a possible escalation— that is, that unsafe behavior is likely, but not necessarily imminent.

5. Identify interventions or strategies to be used by *each* party, at both the red flag and early warning stages.

6. Spell out the specific actions adults will take if the teen engages in unsafe behaviors and doesn't respond to the preventative strategies detailed in this plan.

7. Identify and strategize for any obstacles that may hinder the successful use of this plan.

8. Provide a copy of this plan to your teen, to all adults in the home, and to health providers; if possible, also preview the plan with local law enforcement and emergency service personnel. Having the plan vetted and supported by others will help increase your ability to follow through on it.

Peaceful Parent Practice:
Your Home—A River Runs Through It

A short walk from my front door flows a small waterfall, an offshoot of the Charles River. I've often found myself there when I need a reminder of how much control I *don't* have over what happens in my life. I seem to find myself at the water's edge even more often since I became a dad. I stare at the water moving rapidly over the fall's edge and think, *How am I going to handle this?* and, *Where will the money come from?* and, *This is not what the parenting brochure advertised!*

Sometimes by the waterfall I can catch my mind doing its worrying, regretful, fretful thing and let the thoughts drift away. Standing there, watching the flow of water, I'm reminded of a couple of key facts:

> The angst that brings me to the falls is always different. It's never the exact same mental and emotional landscape.

> Although from one angle the Charles River seems to be a single thing, it's really always changing. For the millionth time I experience and let go into the fact that everything—*everything*—changes.

This Peaceful Parenting Practice is simple, crucial, and yet somehow elusive. Our minds tend to make *things*. We make our lives into various chunks of unchanging granite that we either want or don't want to be permanent. We need the peace that comes from the inevitable truth of change. And as parents of a struggling teen, we want our love for our child to live forever—and yet we also want the pain associated with the teen to make a quick exit. Peace comes from trusting the water-like flow.

In a journal, or just in quiet contemplation, ask yourself: *What outcome am I trying to force—to control—with my teen?* Notice the thoughts and bodily sensations that arise. Notice how you want to either grab or shove away what you're experiencing. Breathe deeply into this impulse and just watch as the thoughts and feelings flow on their own. Watch until you see them change of their own accord. Did you have to force the change? How might you let go of trying to force the chunks of granite that have accumulated around your teen's anger and struggle to change? Can you make letting go your practice and just witness the results as they arrive?

By all means set expectations and limits, express accountability for behavior, and authentically state the impact of your teen's negative behavior on you and others. But do so from the power of a *wu-wei* stance. Let gravity bring the outcomes over which you have no control anyway.

Your Parental Agenda

Before you move on to the next chapter:

- ☐ Look for an opportunity to practice taking a one-down stance with your teen.

- ☐ Identify a specific way you might show curiosity toward your teen—that is, see your teen in a new way—in an upcoming situation. Communicate that to your teen.

- ☐ Practice at least one of the breathing exercises in this chapter and incorporate it into your daily routine.

- ☐ What emotional need do you believe is resting behind your teen's angry behavior? In what concise way can you speak to it? Explore this in your journal.

- ☐ Practice setting compassionate consequences.

- ☐ Create, perhaps with professional support, a home safety plan; discuss it at a family meeting and write it in teen-friendly language.

5 Empowering Change for You and Your Teen

We've arrived at the final PURE step for mindful management of a teen struggling with anger. Hopefully, you've already begun to discover the benefits of practicing skills of mindful presence, both in parenting and in your overall well-being. We've explored the crucial role of compassionate understanding in effective management of tough situations, as well as how both presence and understanding help you to lead effectively. Now, we just have to tie up the interaction! Ideally, you end every parenting exchange with a nudge toward empowering the capacity for change in both you and your teen.

In this chapter you will:

- Build your willingness and skill for self-compassion as you make strides in your parenting.

- Engage in practices designed to amplify your connection with your teen.

- Learn how to build your teen's capacity to assume responsibility for personal behavior.

Self-Compassion: Moving Past Self-Blame

Self-compassion is definitely something you need as a parent of an angry teen. The term has been buzzing around the mindfulness world recently, but what exactly *is* self-compassion? According to experts such as psychotherapist and meditation teacher Tim Desmond (2015), self-compassion involves three primary components: an acknowledgment of the fact of one's own suffering; a recognition of attempts to help oneself; and an acceptance that this suffering is shared with many others—that we're never alone and that there is no true separation from others.

Sounds good, right? In fact, for our lives to be as expansive and free of suffering as possible, we all need heaping doses of self-compassion. Here are some ways to actively practice self-compassion:

Skill Practice: Voice Over

1. Think of a recent mistake or misstep you made while parenting your angry teen.

2. Notice what your inner critic says about you, about how you failed or made things worse, or something else derogatory.

3. Recognize that this critic actually *does* want what's best for you. It's the part of you that wants you to get things right so you avoid causing and experiencing pain.

4. Thank your critic for giving you feedback and for trying to take care of you.

5. Ask yourself what your inner voice might say, and how it might say it, if the same message were delivered in a more compassionate, nonjudgmental tone.

6. Remind yourself of this more compassionate voice whenever the critic rises up in your parenting. Consider writing the compassionate sentiment down on a card or sticky note and placing it where you'll see it throughout the day.

The skill here is to second-guess your second-guessing—to balance yourself with a compassionate acceptance of "errors." In addressing an intense, chronic problem such as teen anger, it's important to remind yourself to focus on progress, not perfection.

Skill Practice: Off the Hook

You are probably aware of some less than ideal habits in your parenting. Perhaps you yell on occasion, or multitask when your teen needs your focused attention, or maybe you lecture your teen too much. Whatever it is, you have some habits like this. We all do.

It's important for all parents—and especially parents with kids who struggle with emotional and behavioral challenges—to cut themselves some slack. If you bought this book, you love your teen. If you're reading it and trying the activities, you're taking this love and using it to build new possibilities for your teen and for you. Let's start with a breathing practice that will soften the hard places in your parental heart.

1. *Breathe in:* notice the pain or upset you've caused by over- or underreacting.

2. *Breathe out:* drop any impulse to beat yourself up yet again.

3. *Breathe in:* allow yourself to begin to forgive yourself.

4. *Breathe out:* connect with your wish for better patterns and less pain for you and your teen.

5. *Breathe in:* a wish for a lightening of the burden of your heart.

Ask Abblett

Q: How am I supposed to have compassion for myself when I'm surrounded by people—my kid in particular—who think I'm screwing everything up? That I'm the source of their misery? How do I let myself off the hook when I'm surrounded by pain and negativity all day, every day?

A: It's said that you are the average of the five people you spend the most time with. Psychologists such as Nicholas Christakis (2004) refer to this as *social contagion* (see chapter 4). While you may not be able to—nor should you—completely divorce yourself from your teen and your teen's angst, you can take a look at the others in your life. Whose positive energy can you spend more time near in the coming days? Notice the effect this has on you and your ability to manage things with more resilience.

Revving Up: Inner Power

We all have habits of mind. However, people vary in their inner responses to a situation—there are different ways to process things. Instead of continuing to practice pain-drenched thinking with regard to your parenting, how about making a daily practice of inside-out empowerment?

Recent data (Creswell et al. 2013) suggests that self-affirmation statements—such as, "This is important to who I am"—can buffer the effects of stress. Here, we'll practice the skill of reconditioning ourselves toward more adaptive modes of self-talk.

Skill Practice: Power Question

1. In your journal, write down one of your strengths as a parent. What is something that you do well as a parent?

2. Sitting in an upright, aware posture with eyes closed, notice what emerges in you with this question. Don't judge, label, or analyze. Simply witness any inner dialogue or reactions.

3. Next, regardless of any chatter from your inner critic, do something that exercises and builds on that strength. Do it right now.

4. Notice how it feels to exercise one of your parenting strengths. Notice the effect this has on your thoughts. How are you handling the situation that arises after having done this? Can you make a regular practice of noticing how it impacts you to perform something well?

5. Try doing this activity soon after or in advance of more challenging parenting situations. Notice the effect of invoking your power in these tougher times.

Skill Practice: Finding FLOW as a Parent of a Teen

You're probably familiar with the idea of being in the zone. Psychologist Mihaly Csikszentmihalyi (1990) calls this *flow*. Flow is a state of energized focus and immersion in an activity that is moderately challenging and for which you have at least moderate skill. You may have noticed yourself in flow while playing your favorite sport or performing an aspect of your work. It feels good to have the experience of time drop away. You flow through an activity with efficiency and effectiveness. When is the last time you experienced flow in your parenting?

Notice what arose for you, in mind and body, upon reading this question. (Return to the preceding section on self-compassion if need be.) It's a safe bet that you are not wholly without skill as a parent— your kid has made it to adolescence after all. It's also likely that there are parenting activities that pose a moderate degree of difficulty for you. The goal here is to be able to identify the match or mismatch between your skill and the activity's difficulty, and then to address any gaps.

1. In a single column your journal, list the activities you engage in regularly as a parent that pose very little challenge (e.g. for the color blind/challenged like me, doing the laundry). Now

list activities that are extremely challenging (e.g. speaking compassionately behind a teen's nasty, acting out behavior). Next, list activities that appear to fall in the moderate range of challenge to you.

2. In an adjacent column, honestly assess how skilled you are in performing each of these activities. Try to be as objective as possible. Get feedback from someone you trust to gauge your accuracy.

3. Next, scan your list for well-matched pairs—where your skills nicely match the challenge of the activity, particularly moderate ones. Schedule yourself to do at least one of these activities in the next twenty-four hours. Reflect—perhaps journal—about your inner experience of doing this activity. How does it feel to do it? How does it impact things later in your day, particularly with regard to your interactions with your teen and your practice of the other skills in this book?

4. Identify the parenting activities that are highly challenging and currently appear to exceed your skill levels. Consider pursuing resources—books, clinicians, other professionals, a trusted mentor or family member—in order to build your skills in these areas. Remember: progress not perfection. Is the activity important enough for moving things forward with your teen that you're willing to put in the time, effort, and money to beef up your skill? Note any inner or outer obstacles you may experience and develop a plan for addressing them.

5. Do a passion check on your parenting. Whether it's the activity you've listed above or another altogether, what parenting activity are you willing to do—today—without any pay, praise, or prompting from another? What could you do with absolute, undivided attention? Flow into that right now.

From Garbage to Flowers

Any organic gardener intuitively knows what meditation teacher Thich Nhat Hanh (1991) means when he says that you cannot have flowers without garbage. The best flowers grow out of healthy doses of compost—garbage. And compost or garbage is, of course, what all flowers eventually become. Nhat Hanh reminds us of what at some level we already know: bad things can lead to good things, and good things themselves inevitably change.

Pain can become possibility. This is not just a greeting card sentiment. But in order for this to happen, we need to be open to experiencing pain. Empowering change with your teen requires being aware of the changing tides of pain. Instead of seeing the pain of things with your teen as stone solid, can you get curious as to how it has, is, and will certainly always change?

Skill Practice: Gratitude Breathing

1. Sitting upright with your eyes closed, call to mind a recent interaction with your teen that went extremely well, where you connected or shared in something meaningful or fun.

2. As the image of this situation appears, notice the sensations in your body.

3. For ten breaths, sit with that image and any sensations or thoughts that arise.

4. Count each breath gently and silently, keeping your focus on the experience of that good time.

5. Open your eyes and notice how you feel. Truly savor this experience for its beauty.

Now, repeat these steps a second time. This time call to mind a recent exchange with your teen that did *not* go well, one that may have involved considerable intensity and pain for both of you. Notice what arises. Stay with this as you count out ten breaths. Don't worry about breathing in any particular way, simply notice the breath moving in and out as you focus on the images and sensations from the situation.

Ask yourself: At the close of just these ten breaths, have the images and sensations of this tough episode remained exactly the same in quality and content? Have they changed on their own?

Ask yourself: How might the "garbage" of this episode continue to change across ongoing, mindful breaths? Over ten thousand breaths? Is there anything you or your teen can learn from this situation? Do you feel any more resolve to improve things? How might this garbage transform with time into a flower?

Attunement to Your Angry Teen

In a famous series of studies (Tronick et al. 1978), developmental psychologist Ed Tronick asked parents to cease their typical back-and-forth interactions with their infants and abruptly face them instead with blank expressions. Through these "still face" experiments, Tronick documented the immense impact—physiological, psychological, and behavioral—of interrupting the normal dance of emotional attunement, impact that was felt by both the baby and the parent.

You know this already because you feel the impact of the disrupted flow of emotional give and take with your teen. And, of course, your teen feels it as well. Tronick showed that these interruptions significantly impact the stress levels—and therefore the development—of an infant. For the wellbeing of you and your teen, it's important to shift the emotional balance back toward attunement.

Ask Abblett

Q: I don't believe that my daughter cares about connecting with me. How am I supposed to believe that she gives a damn when all I get is her anger and resentment? When all I get is blamed for everything that's not going well for her?

A: The opposite of love is not hate. As a supervisor of mine said long ago, it's really something more akin to indifference. When teens give you their anger, they are giving you a message of their pain—a message that they want you to hear. They are still children who want their parents to help remove the pain. We often make those we love most the targets of our anger because really we're searching for more connection.

Skill Practice: Hang Time

Whether it's inane gossip shows about overexposed and overpaid celebrities or video games that require more manual dexterity than piloting a fighter jet, it's time you got comfortable hanging out with your teen. The point here is to make deposits in your teen's emotional bank account that you can draw on later. You want to give small experiences of dedicated attention. Attunement and emotional investment in favorite activities will help your teen care more about your relationship going forward. Improvements in the parent–child relationship will increase the prospect for your teen to get on top of all that anger.

Your willingness to hang out with full attention and engagement will help your teen develop the resilience to hang in there with the difficulties of the change process. Try these steps:

1. Carve out at least ten to fifteen minutes per day to hang out with your teen. If possible, establish a regular time for hanging out, a time when you are free from other responsibilities or competing demands.

2. Express interest in joining your teen in some sort of leisure activity at home. Don't force the issue. If the teen refuses to allow you to even sit nearby, simply state something like, "Okay, well I'd really like to hang out with you, so I'll look to check-in with you later." And then follow up, even if it takes twenty rejections before your teen finally says, "whatever" and allows you to sit nearby while your kid plays *Grand Theft Auto*. If your teen suggests you're just trying to spy or get into the teen's business, then say something like, "Hey, I'm just trying to flip things around between you and me. I just want to show some interest in what matters to you."

3. Ideally, the teen is up for doing something interactive with you, such as a game. If not, just sit as your teen does whatever it is your teen likes to do.

4. Avoid asking questions. Again, your teen will likely assume that you're prying, or perhaps judging in some way. Avoid lecturing or trying to teach. This is *not* a time to instruct your teen in any way. Don't try to direct or manage how your teen does the activity. Also, don't inquire into sensitive topics during hangout time. The focus here is not the content of any hot button issues—it's on the process of your communication with each other.

5. Practice attunement by:

    • Praising your teen's specific actions and positive communication with you. For example, "Nice job clearing that level in the game." Or, "It's cool how you asked if I wanted to take a crack at this."

    • Summarize anything your teen says that indicates engagement, even if that's engagement with the activity or topic rather than with you. For example, "So, I'm hearing you say that most people don't have a clue of how good you are at this."

- Describe what your teen is doing as if you're a correspondent doing a radio broadcast for a sporting event. For example, "Looks like you're done watching the Kardashians, and now it's time to get down to business with some Xbox action."

6. Let your teen lead the interaction. Practice letting go of trying to control things. Suppress any disdain for your teen's preferences or passion for what *you* see as an irrational, nonsensical activity. Remember, your teen expects you to show disapproval or sit in judgment. It will send a very powerful message—a message your teen will certainly detect—if you refrain from doing so.

Skill Practice: SAVORing with the Breath

Here's another activity for creating more positivity in your relationship with your teen. This activity has less to do with shifting the dynamics of communication between you, and more to do with shifting your own internal stance. The activity helps spark remembrances of good times and affinity with your teen. These then ripple into your daily life.

1. **S**it quietly with a favorite memento from a good time with your teen. This could be a stub from a film you enjoyed together, a favorite toy you gave your teen at the holidays, anything.

2. **A**llow all of your senses to engage the object (perhaps not taste!).

3. **V**alue the pleasant sensations and thoughts—the peace—that arise.

4. **O**pen to any and all possibilities of transfering this peace to other situations today, whether that's in interactions with your teen or not.

5. **R**est in what you cherish about this time with your teen.

The next time you're in an actual interaction with your teen that involves some fun or meaningfulness, try savoring it. In the midst of the experience, take at least five conscious breaths. Gently count the breaths to yourself as you take in what is wonderful about the situation. What happens to your experience of your teen as you willingly breathe into it?

_____

Inviting the Choice to Change

A large body of research reveals that people are more likely to do the hard work of changing difficult behaviors when they believe they are choosing to do so (Prochaska and DiClemente 1983; Deci and Ryan 2000). Whether it's addressing addictions, following through on healthy lifestyle choices, or heeding a doctor's recommendations, a sense of autonomy is crucial to the change process.

Change is not easy for most of us. For teens with anger issues, change can be particularly challenging. It's important to empower teens to *choose* the changes their lives require.

Pause and think about your own change-resistant behaviors from the past. Perhaps it was smoking, unhealthy eating patterns, or even a nail-biting habit. Did you change when you felt pressured to by others? When you felt down and out? You likely changed only when you felt yourself at the helm, not when you felt pushed from behind.

_____

Skill Practice: Real Choices

Let's assume you've set a limit on your teen's behavior. Perhaps you've grounded your teen for having given you the finger in front of dinner guests. You waited until after your guests left to address the issue, to lower the intensity for you and your teen. Following the steps for compassionate consequences in chapter 4, you went to the doorway of your teen's room and stated the consequence for the teen's behavior. Now you need to end the interaction with a brief reminder of your teen's ability to choose:

1. Assuming it is physically safe to say anything further after setting the limit, prepare yourself by softening your demeanor. With a full belly breath, relax your facial expressions and consciously ease the tension in your body.

2. Look at your teen. Speaking more softly than when you set the limit, directly state, "What happens next is entirely up to you. You get to decide how you handle this."

3. Check your tone. Be sincere, not sarcastic. Do not, in any way, taunt your teen with a "let's see how you handle this" edge.

4. Offer to assist your teen with something that neither diminishes nor negates the consequence you've set. For example, if you've taken away your teen's cell phone, that doesn't mean you can't offer to get the teen a glass of water. Your willingness to be civil and sincere will help debunk any suspicions that you're rejecting or demeaning the teen as a person. You dislike the behavior, not the person.

Eyeing the Prize in Your Teen

Teens can respond well to praise from the adults in their lives. They can also react negatively if they feel they're being praised so as to manipulate them into doing something the adult wants, or they perceive the praise as inauthentic. A helpful alternative to praising is the concept of *prizing* behavior. Prizing is a relationship-building skill that lets teens know their efforts are noticed. Prizing models authenticity and helps teens build their resilience and capacity to hang in there with challenges.

Here are a couple of additional advantages of prizing: it makes you—and your perspective and feelings—matter more to your teen.

Your teen will thus be more likely to take input and direction from you. Prizing is also contagious. It builds a culture of connection.

Skill Practice: Prizing vs. Praising

1. Anticipate upcoming interactions. Ask yourself: *How can I let my teen know that I recognize a valuable trait or effort?* Maybe this would be through a direct comment in which you let your teen know you've noticed something really cool. Maybe it's a gesture where you thank your teen for showing this side.

2. Prize with patience. Get eye-level, be sincere, and let your teen know about the valuable effort or behavior you see. Be patient. Your teen may not respond readily, or even at all. For teens with low self-esteem, positive input can feel discrepant with how they view themselves. They may reject what you're doing or saying altogether. Don't give up! If they're used to people giving up, giving up now is only likely to confirm the script they've been acting out. Through consistent prizing, show them a new script is possible.

3. Let go of your own agendas, your own need for kudos. You're the adult; your teen is the kid. Find your thank-yous and congratulations elsewhere. Trust that the message, when given enthusiastically and authentically, will resonate even if your teen doesn't acknowledge it openly. This is not something your teen needs to be polite about. When you're planting seeds, it doesn't make sense to get mad that a seed doesn't immediately bear fruit.

4. Here's an acronym to help you remember the keys points for effective prizing with your teen—or with anyone for that matter. Try it out with others in your circle and notice the effects:

 · **P**resence

Respectful framing of the other

Interconnectedness and mutual impact

Zero agenda

Empowerment and enabling autonomy

Ask Abblett

Q: I really don't feel like prizing my teen. He is so negative and draining. He does so little that I can be proud of—how am I supposed to honestly prize him? Won't it make things worse to be fake?

A: Yes, being fake will certainly not help things. Your teen will see through it and resent you all the more. The trick is to keep working to see behind your teen's angry behavior. Is there any aspect of resilience in him? Has there been any—even the smallest—effort on his part to try to show the world something other than anger? This could be a supportive gesture for a friend, or putting grungy clothes in the hamper without being asked. Prizing is about reflecting authentic effort with a genuine message of respect and valuing. It doesn't matter how small that effort is.

Peaceful Parent Practice: Stressus Interruptus

This practice is deceptively simple. Its key lies in the cueing—in remembering and actually following through in the heat of things.

1. Anticipate a likely conflict with your teen in the coming days. What marker or signal tends to happen that indicates a blowup is imminent? This could be your teen's angry glare, your own clenching throat, or a knot in your stomach.

2. Create a specific cue or reminder primed to guide you during an impending conflict. For example, this could be an index card with the word "interrupt" written on it. In your mind, link the cue with the marker or signal you identified in the previous step. Place this cue in a spot where you'll see it as a conflict is developing with your teen.

3. Identify a short but effective strategy you've used previously to calm and take care of yourself. Some examples are: listening to music, taking a bath, working out, going for a walk, drinking a cup of tea.

4. Plan so that, the moment a blowup seems imminent during an actual interaction, you will interrupt your own behavior and put your self-care strategy into action. Do this no matter how much your inner engine churns for further reactivity.

5. Before exiting the interaction, look at your teen and say something like, "I know this is very important to you, and I also know I need a break. I'll be back later to see if you want to work this out. Right now, I'm going to go slow things down. I will be back."

6. Be certain to circle back. Do not prescribe, recommend, preach, or in any way lecture how your *teen* should be calming down. Let your actions speak on their own.

Your Parental Agenda

Before you move on to the next chapter:

- ☐ Select a self-compassion practice for when you get stuck in blaming yourself. Use it.

- ☐ Practice one of your parental strengths.

- ☐ Contemplate the "garbage" and how it might flower or is already flowering.

- ☐ Commit to hanging out with your teen on a daily basis.

- ☐ Develop and maintain a practice of prizing effort and change-related risk-taking in your teen.

Conclusion: Bringing It All Together with the PURE Method

We've now advanced through all four steps of the PURE method. Along the way, you've done a lot of practicing. As we wrap up the book and our time together, I want to point out the "pure" does not mean perfect. As writer Kurt Vonnegut told an auditorium of us aspiring authors many years ago, "you *will* fail." And, yes, you have failed and will fail as a parent. The best results come for parents who let go of trying to force results to happen (remember *wu-wei* from chapter 4?). Pure is not perfection; it's moving forward, with purpose and intention, toward what matters most about you, your teen, and your relationship.

Before we close, let's explore how to integrate the PURE skills fluidly. It won't work to tell your angry teen, "Wait, I need to check to see what it says I should do in chapter 2. I'll get back to you and your rant in a few minutes." You need a sense not just of the *how* of these skills, but of the *when* as well.

Matching PURE Skills to the Moment at Hand

Accurate timing is crucial to effectively responding to your teen's behavioral struggles and the emotional turbulence that affects the entire household. Highly skilled technical professionals like athletes and surgeons have to hone their sense of timing—small miscalculations can lead to negative outcomes ranging from lost games to lost lives.

Think about it: How would you feel if your surgeon told you in the pre-op room that she was just going to wing it? That she planned to cut you open and then just address any problems that crop up? We expect certainty and skill in a surgeon's timing. We should aspire to high standards in our parental timing as well. Arguably, there's as much at stake in parenting as in many an operating room.

To stack the deck in favor of better timing in your use of the PURE skills, consider these questions:

- Whose agenda or needs are the focus in this moment? Mine, my teen's, or others'?

- Am I open and aware of what's happening inside and around me?

- Does what I'm about to do really matter? Is it rooted in my core values and aspirations as a parent? Would my next move be one I will in no way regret in my dying moments?

- What message will my behavior send?

Skill Practice: Listen, Look, and Leap

Most of us aren't trained prior to parenthood to smoothly time our attempts to manage kids' problem behaviors. That's okay—the following sequence will help you get a better sense of the *when* of parenting, particularly in dealing with tough exchanges with an unhappy teen. Such stuck moments are ripe for a Relational Compass check (see chapter 3). Here are the steps:

1. *Listen* to what your body and thoughts are doing. As we practiced in chapter 2, notice and allow any critical or rigid thoughts to pass through you. Notice any bodily sensations of

tightening or surging; let the currents of this energy die away on their own.

2. *Look* to your compass headings. What directions or themes of action matter to you? Perhaps, for example, deeply connecting, being real, or modeling courage for your kids. Don't just think about these. Feel the pull of them.

3. *Leap!* Choose a behavior that is consistent with one of these headings and seems to fit the situation you're in. Move toward it—and do it! Do it despite whatever your inner critic says.

Coaches Can't Quit

I hated Little League when I was a kid—I wasn't good at it and was desperately afraid of being laughed at by my peers. Still, the option to quit came with my glove and uniform. Though it wasn't an ideal step, I could always just walk off the field. And I did.

Coaches don't have that same option to quit. Captains go down with ships and coaches rise and fall with their teams. They don't walk off the field and leave their teams literally holding the ball.

As a parent of a troubled teen, you may feel like quitting on a regular—maybe even daily—basis. Don't deny the truth and pain of this feeling. At the same time, don't make the mistake of believing that you have the option of quitting. You are your teen's coach. You are a true mentor for your teen's emotional self.

Ask Abblett

Q: What about *my* feelings? My life? Don't I have the right to take care of myself at some point? Shouldn't they be responsible for their own choices by the time they're a teen? Why can't we just agree that they need something other than what I can give them?

A: Yes, you have the right to take care of yourself, but the goal should be to do so in a way that keeps your well-being *and your teen's* at the forefront. Whether you walk away or lean in, you are coaching your teen. Physical presence or absence does not change this fact. As parents we are always sending emotional messages to our children.

Maintaining Your Momentum

After my daughter was born, I remember going for a run outside the hospital to clear my head. I felt so overwhelmed and intimidated by this new parenthood "thing." I literally felt like running away.

Not far from the hospital was Boston's Museum of Fine Arts. I stopped at the sight of Cyrus Dallin's 1909 bronze statue, *Appeal to the Great Spirit*. I'd seen this statue, which stands at the front of the museum, many times. The statue depicts a Native American warrior, with arms outstretched, gaze skyward. This time, however, I shared the warrior's sentiment—I felt I needed to call on a power greater than myself to be able to address the challenge before me.

I've learned since that there's a great deal within each of us that we can call upon to make it through the challenges of parenting. Take a moment to reflect on the following questions as you make your way forward:

- When was the last time you thought you couldn't keep going but then did? When might be the next time?

- When times are hardest, do you tend to look outside yourself for motivation? This isn't inherently bad. In fact, family, friends, and higher powers are crucial to parenting. But here, now, ask yourself: *As I look inside myself, what matters most with regard to my teen and my family?*

Finally, try the following steps to help make the PURE skills a more fluid, daily part of your parenting. This sequence outlines the core process for integrating these psychological, emotional, and behavioral skills into who you are:

1. *Seeing the change*: Identify a model. Who is someone you admire who has demonstrated proficiency with the PURE skill you're working on? Make this person your internal surrogate. Visualize how this person would handle specific situations using the skill you're looking to develop. Imagine the person performing this action in vivid sensory detail. Next, try on similar behaviors: visualize replacing this surrogate with yourself and watch the mental movie of yourself mastering this skill.

2. *Doing the change*: Even if your performance falls short of your visualization, put the PURE skill into action at the next available opportunity. Don't be down on yourself for any perceived failure. Use mindfulness to wade through such reactions.

3. *Reviewing the change*: Track your progress in a journal. Get regular feedback on your development of the skill from those you trust to be brutally yet compassionately honest with you.

4. *Being the change*: Integrate this skill into a new definition of your parenting. Don't view this skill as merely a behavior pattern you adopted. View it as part of who you are as a parent specifically and as a person more generally. Celebrate your progress. Give yourself the credit you deserve for this work on behalf of your family.

Working with Professionals

Professionals vary in what they recommend for addressing the anger problems of a teen, even with regard to some of the points in this book. Don't allow this inconsistency to dissuade you from seeking help from a licensed clinical provider. Whether it be family or couples therapy, parent guidance/training, medication, or individual therapy for yourself, take advantage of the well-documented fact that a strong alliance with a provider helps produce the best treatment outcomes. If you find any of the PURE skills difficult to develop or implement, or simply insufficient to the situation you're facing, professional assistance can be enormously valuable. Even when this book helps you make strides, a clinician can help you deepen and extend this progress further.

And beyond skill development, raising a child struggling with anger takes a huge toll on the well-being of any parent. A therapist can help you come to terms with the pain and loss you've experienced.

Peaceful Parent Practice:
Learned Hopefulness

Let's end by revisiting a well-researched principle we first explored in chapter 1. Psychologist Carol Dweck (2006) has shown that the mindset we adopt when facing obstacles determines whether we believe that we can learn and grow or if we believe that outcomes are set in stone by uncontrollable external factors. We approach life with either a growth mindset or a fixed mindset. This mindset impacts our willingness and capacity for change. Further, Dweck's research points to how our children's mindsets are strongly influenced by our own. Our children are the heirs not only of our actions, but of our mindset as well.

In your journal, contemplate how:

- You will continue to develop yourself as a parent.

- The challenges you face are opportunities for growth.

- You can sidestep judgments and disasters and stop avoiding the very aspects of your family life that, if you leaned into them, might open up possibilities.

The next time you walk into the room with your teen, set an intention for the fresh possibilities that the coming moments will bring. Setting this intention—and being willing to do so over and over again despite failure—will move you forward into pure connection with your teen.

Acknowledgments

First and foremost, I could not have written about parenting without the immensely positive and loving parenting I myself received. My parents have given me the foundation not only for my professional life as a clinician but also for my personal life as a parent. Intergenerational transmission isn't just about negative behaviors—it's also about the gifts we inherit from the generations before.

Many others also have my unending gratitude for directly or indirectly shaping and shepherding this book. I owe an incredible debt to my many clients—parents, children, or otherwise—who have trusted me with their pain and inspired me with their courage. Many colleagues have contributed ideas, feedback, and encouragement along the way. My friends at the Institute for Meditation and Psychotherapy (IMP) have been an ongoing source of support. I'm thankful to my fellow authors and mindfulness aficionados (Dzung Vo, Susan Kaiser-Greenland, Mark Bertin, Elisha Goldstein, and Steve Hickman), who gave of their time and expertise to review and comment on this book. In particular, I owe immense thanks to my friend, colleague, and mindful partner in crime, Dr. Chris Willard. Chris, your energy, intellect, and grace are indirectly reflected in much of my writing and speaking these days.

I owe, too, a great debt of thanks to my wife, Lisa, and our two children, Celia and Theo. Your patience and support as I place my attention on projects other than my daily sharing with you is a gift I can never fully repay. I promise to give you more of my presence, in every sense of the word.

Lastly, a big thank you to the team at New Harbinger (Jess O'Brien, Clancy Drake, Jesse Burson, and Amy Johnson) for consistently doing the good work of turning ideas and words into books with the potential to impact a wide swath of people.

All parents deserve compassion and peace. The pains of parenthood are universal to us all. Let's not allow such pains to drown out the beauty of what we've brought into the world.

References

Abblett, M. 2013. *The Heat of the Moment in Treatment: Mindful Management of Difficult Clients*. New York: W. W. Norton.

Achor, S. 2010. *The Happiness Advantage*. New York: Crown Business.

Baumeister, R., and J. Tierney. 2012. *Willpower: Rediscovering the Greatest Human Strength*. New York: Penguin.

Barkley, R., and A. L. Robin. 2013. *The Defiant Teen: 10 Steps to Resolve Conflict and Build Your Relationships*, 2nd edition. New York: Guilford Press.

Biswas-Diener, R., T. B. Kashdan, and G. Minhas. 2011. "A Dynamic Approach to Psychological Strength Development and Intervention." *Journal of Positive Psychology* 6: 106–118.

Brown, K. W. and R. M. Ryan. 2003. "The Benefits of Being Present: Mindfulness and Its Role in Psychological Well-Being." *Journal of Personality and Social Psychology* 84: 822–848.

Chaffin, M., J. F. Silovsky, B. Funderburk, L. A. Valle, E. V. Brestan, T. Balachova, S. Jackson, J. Lensgraf, and B. L. Bonner. 2004. "Parent–Child Interaction Therapy with Physically Abusive Parents: Efficacy for Reducing Future Abuse Reports." *Journal of Consulting and Clinical Psychology* 72: 500–510.

Chorpita, B. F., and J. R. Weisz. 2009. *Modular Approach to Therapy for Children with Anxiety, Depression, Trauma, or Conduct Problems (MATCH–ADTC)*. Satellite Beach, FL: PracticeWise.

Christakis, N. A., and J. H. Fowler. 2011. *Connected: The Surprising Power of Our Social Networks and How They Shape Our Lives*. New York: Back Bay Books.

Christakis, N. A. 2004. "Social Networks and Collateral Health Effects." *British Medical Journal* 329: 184–185.

Creswell, J. D., J. M. Dutcher, W. M. P. Klein, P. R. Harris, and J. M. Levine. 2013. "Self-Affirmation Improves Problem-Solving Under Stress." *PLoS ONE* 8(5): e62593.

Csikszentmihalyi, M. 1990. *Flow: The Psychology of Optimal Experience.* New York: Harper.

———. 1998. *Finding Flow: The Psychology of Engagement with Everyday Life.* New York: Basic Books.

Dawe, S., and P. Harnett. 2007. "Potential for Child Abuse Among Methadone-Maintained Parents: Results from a Randomized Controlled Trial." *Journal of Substance Abuse Treatment* 32: 381–390.

Deci, E. L., and R. M. Ryan. 2000. "Self-Determination Theory and the Facilitation of Intrinsic Motivation, Social Development and Well-Being." *American Psychologist* 55: 68–78.

Desmond, T. 2015. *Self-Compassion in Psychotherapy: Mindfulness-Based Practices for Healing and Transformation.* New York: W. W. Norton.

Dishion, T. J., S. E. Nelson, and B. M. Bullock. 2004. "Premature Adolescent Autonomy: Parent Disengagement and Deviant Peer Process in the Amplification of Problem Behavior." *Journal of Adolescence* 27: 515–530.

Duckworth, A., C. Peterson, M. Matthews, and D. Kelly. 2007. "Grit: Perseverance and Passion for Long-Term Goals." *Journal of Personality and Social Psychology* 92: 1087–1101.

Duffy, A., and J. Momirov. 2000. "Family Violence: Issues and Advances at the End of the Twentieth Century." In *Canadian Families*, 2nd ed., edited by N. Mandell and A. Duffy. Toronto: Harcourt Brace Canada.

Duncan, L. G., J. D. Coatsworth, and M. T. Greenberg. 2009. "A Model of Mindful Parenting: Implications for Parent-Child

Relationships and Prevention Research." *Clinical Child and Family Psychological Review* 12: 255–270

Dweck, C. 2006. *Mindset: The New Psychology of Success.* New York: Ballantine.

Eliot, T. S. 1964. *Murder in the Cathedral.* New York: Harcourt.

Gandhi, M. K. (1951) 2001. *Non-Violent Resistance (Satyagraha).* New York: Schocken Books. Reprint, Mineola, NY: Dover Publications.

Gilbert, D., and P. S. Malone. 1995. "The Correspondence Bias." *Psychological Bulletin* 117: 21–38.

Goleman, D. 2007. *Social Intelligence: The New Science of Human Relationships.* New York: Bantam.

Gottman, J., and S. Carrere. 1999. "Predicting Divorce Among Newly-Weds from the First Three Minutes of a Marital Conflict Discussion." *Family Process* 38: 293–301.

Gottman, J. M., L. F. Katz, and C. Hooven. 1996. "Parental Meta-Emotion Philosophy and the Emotional Life of Families: Theoretical Models and Preliminary Data." *Journal of Family Psychology* 10(3): 243–268.

Granic, I., and G. R. Patterson. 2006. "Toward a Comprehensive Model of Antisocial Development: A Dynamic Systems Approach." *Psychological Review* 113: 101–131.

Grossman, P., L. Niemann, S. Schmidt, and H. Walach. 2004. "Mindfulness-Based Stress Reduction and Health Benefits: A Meta-Analysis." *Journal of Psychosomatic Research* 57: 35–43.

Gyatso, T. 2010. "Ten Questions for the Dalai Lama." *Time.* June 14.

Hakim-Larson, J., A. Parker, C. Lee, and S. Voelker. 2006. "Measuring Parental Meta-Emotion: Psychometric Properties of the Emotion-Related Parenting Styles Self-Test." *Early Education and Development*, 17: 229–251.

Halberstadt, A. G., V. W. Crisp, and K. L. Eaton. 1999. "Family Expressiveness: A Retrospective and New Directions for Research." In *The Social Context of Nonverbal Behavior: Studies in Emotion and Social Interaction*, edited by P. Philippot and R. S. Feldman. New York: Cambridge University Press.

Hayes, S. C., K. D. Strosahl, and K. G. Wilson. 2011. *Acceptance and Commitment Therapy: The Process and Practice of Mindful Change*, 2nd ed. New York: Guilford Press.

Hoffman, S. G., A. T. Sawyer, A. A. Witt, and D. Oh. 2010. "The Effect of Mindfulness-Based Therapy on Anxiety and Depression: A Meta-Analytic Review." *Journal of Consulting and Clinical Psychology* 78: 169–183.

Kabat-Zinn, J. 2003. "Mindfulness-Based Enterventions in Context: Past, Present and Future." *Clinical Psychology: Science and Practice* 10: 144–156.

———. 2013. *Full Catastrophe Living: Using the Wisdom of Your Body and Mind to Face Stress, Pain, and Illness.* New York: Bantam.

Kaminski, W., L. A. Valle, and J. H. Filene. 2008. "A Meta-Analytic Review of Components Associated with Parent Training Program Effectiveness." *Journal of Abnormal Child Psychology* 36: 567.

Klein, D. C., E. Fencil-Morse, and M. E. P. Seligman. 1976. "Learned Helplessness, Depression, and the Attribution of Failure." *Journal of Personality and Social Psychology* 33: 508–516.

Kornfield, J. 1993. *A Path with Heart.* New York: Bantam.

Lazar, S. W., G. Bush, R. L. Gollub, G. L. Fricchione, G. Khalsa, and H. Benson. 2000. "Functional Brain Mapping of the Relaxation Response and Meditation." *Neuroreport* 11: 1581–1585.

Linley, A. 2008. *Average to A-plus: Realizing Strengths in Yourself and Others.* Coventry, UK: CAPP Press.

Masten, A. S., and J. D. Coatsworth. 1998. "The Development of Competence in Favorable and Unfavorable Environments: Lessons from Research on Successful Children." *American Psychologist* 53: 205–220.

McLeod, K. 2002. *Wake Up to Your Life: Discovering the Buddhist Path of Attention.* New York: HarperOne.

Merikangas, K. R., J. P. He, D. Brody, P. W. Fisher, K. Bourdon, and D. S. Koretz. 2010. "Prevalence and Treatment of Mental Disorders among US Children in the 2001–2004 NHANES." *Pediatrics* 125: 75–81.

Murray, W. H. 1951. *The Scottish Himalayan Expedition.* New York: J. M. Dent & Co.

Nhat Hanh, T. 1999. *The Miracle of Mindfulness: An Introduction to the Practice of Meditation.* Boston: Beacon Press.

———. 1991. *Peace Is Every Step: The Path of Mindfulness in Everyday Life.* New York: Bantam.

Obsuth, I., M. M. Morette, R. Holland, K. Braber, and S. Cross. 2006. "Conduct Disorder: New Directions in Promoting Effective Parenting and Strengthening Parent-Aadolescent Relationships." *Journal of the Canadian Academy of Child and Adolescent Psychiatry* 15: 6–15.

Patterson, G. R. 1982. *A Social Learning Approach: Coercive Family Process.* Eugene, OR: Castalia.

Prochaska, J., and C. DiClemente. 1983. "Stages and Processes of Self-Change in Smoking: Toward an Integrative Model of Change." *Journal of Consulting and Clinical Psychology* 5: 390–395.

Schneider, W. J., T. A. Cavell, and J. N. Hughes. 2003. "A Sense of Containment: Potential Moderator of the Relation Between Parenting Practices and Children's Externalizing Behaviors." *Development and Psychopathology* 15: 95–117.

Seigel, D. J., and M. Hartzell. 2004. *Parenting from the Inside Out: How a Deeper Self-Understanding Can Help You Raise Children Who Thrive.* New York: J. P. Tarcher/Penguin.

Seligman, M. E. P. 2002. *Authentic Happiness: Using the New Positive Psychology to Realize Potential for Lasting Fulfillment.* New York: Free Press.

———. 2006. "Afterword: Breaking the 65 percent Barrier." In *A Life Worth Living: Contributions to Positive Psychology,* edited by M. Csikszentmihalyi and I. S. Csikszentmihalyi. New York: Oxford University Press. 230–236.

Simpson, J. A., W. A. Collins, S. Tran, and K. C. Hayden. 2007. "Attachment and the Experience and Expression of Emotion in Romantic Relationships: A Developmental Perspective." *Journal of Personality and Social Psychology* 92: 355–367.

Stettler, N., and L. F. Katz. 2014. "Changes in Parents Meta-Emotion Philosophy from Preschool to Early Adolescence." *Parenting: Science and Practice* 14: 162–174.

Tronick, E., H. Als, L. Adamson, S. Wise, and T. B. Brazelton. 1978. "Infants' Response to Entrapment Between Contradictory Messages in Face-to-Face Interaction." *Journal of the American Academy of Child and Adolescent Psychiatry* 17: 1–13.

Tzu, L. 2012. *Tao Te Ching,* translated by T. Butler-Bowdon. Hoboken, NJ: Capstone.

Uchino, B. N. 2004. "Understanding the Links Between Wocial Support and Physical Health." *Perspectives on Psychological Science* 4: 236–255.

Vestergaard-Paulsen, P., M. van Beek, J. Skewes, C. R. Bjarkam, M. Stubberup, J. Bertelsen, and A. Roepstorff. 2009. "Long-Term Meditation is Associated with Increased Gray Matter Density in the Brain Stem." *Neuroreport* 20: 170–174.

Wilson, E. O. 2004. *On Human Nature.* Cambridge, MA: Harvard University Press.

Mitch R. Abblett, PhD, is a clinical psychologist and executive director of The Institute for Meditation and Psychotherapy, a non-profit focusing on education and training at the intersection of mindfulness and treatment. For over a decade, he was clinical director of the Manville School, a Harvard-affiliated therapeutic day school program in Boston, MA, serving children with emotional, behavioral, and learning difficulties. He maintains a private psychotherapy and consulting practice (www.drmitchabblett.com), and writes about mindfulness, professional development, and family mental health. His books include *The Heat of the Moment in Treatment* (W.W. Norton) for clinicians, *Mindfulness for Teen Depression* (New Harbinger, coauthored with Chris Willard, PsyD), and the upcoming *Overcoming the Five Hindrances to Awakened Living* (Shambhala Publications). He also coauthored the child/family friendly practice aid *Growing Mindful*, as well as additional mindfulness-related card decks. He conducts national and international trainings regarding mindfulness and its applications.

Foreword writer **Christopher Willard, PsyD**, is a psychologist and educational consultant based in Boston, MA, specializing in mindfulness. He has been practicing meditation for over fifteen years, and leads workshops internationally on the topic of mindfulness for treating young people. He currently serves on the board of directors at the Institute for Meditation and Psychotherapy, and the Mindfulness in Education Network. His thoughts on mental health have been featured in *The New York Times*, on cnn.com, and elsewhere. Willard is author of *Child's Mind*, *Growing Up Mindful*, and three other books. He teaches on the faculty of Harvard Medical School.

MORE BOOKS *from*
NEW HARBINGER PUBLICATIONS

ENDING THE PARENT-TEEN CONTROL BATTLE

Resolve the Power Struggle & Build Trust, Responsibility & Respect

ISBN 978-1626254244 / US 16.95

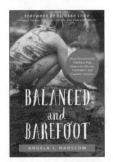

BALANCED & BAREFOOT

How Unrestricted Outdoor Play Makes for Strong, Confident & Capable Children

ISBN 978-1626253735 / US $16.95

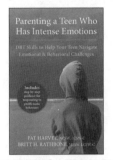

PARENTING A TEEN WHO HAS INTENSE EMOTIONS

DBT Skills to Help Your Teen Navigate Emotional & Behavioral Challenges

ISBN 978-1626251885 / US $16.95

TRANSFORMING STRESS FOR TEENS

The HeartMath® Solution for Staying Cool Under Pressure

ISBN 978-1626251946 / US $16.95

THE ANGER WORKBOOK FOR TEENS

Activities to Help You Deal with Anger & Frustration

ISBN 978-1572246997 / US $15.95

DON'T LET YOUR EMOTIONS RUN YOUR LIFE FOR TEENS

Dialectical Behavior Therapy Skills for Helping You Manage Mood Swings, Control Angry Outbursts & Get Along with Others

ISBN 978-1572248830 / US $16.95

Instant Help Books
An Imprint of New Harbinger Publications

newharbingerpublications
1-800-748-6273 / newharbinger.com

(VISA, MC, AMEX / prices subject to change without notice)

Follow Us

Don't miss out on new books in the subjects that interest you.
Sign up for our **Book Alerts** at **newharbinger.com/bookalerts**

Register your **new harbinger** titles for additional benefits!

When you register your **new harbinger** title— purchased in any format, from any source—you get access to benefits like the following:

- Downloadable accessories like printable worksheets and extra content

- Instructional videos and audio files

- Information about updates, corrections, and new editions

Not every title has accessories, but we're adding new material all the time.

Access free accessories in 3 easy steps:

1. Sign in at NewHarbinger.com (or **register** to create an account).

2. Click on **register a book**. Search for your title and click the **register** button when it appears.

3. Click on the **book cover or title** to go to its details page. Click on **accessories** to view and access files.

That's all there is to it!

If you need help, visit:

NewHarbinger.com/accessories

new harbinger
CELEBRATING
4O YEARS